"If the end of your marriage feels lik[...] will prove a timely rescue for your heart. With refreshing transparency, practical advice, and engaging humor, Betsy gently guides you from deep hurt to deep hope through God's boundless love."

Allen Arnold, executive producer of content at Wild at Heart and author of *The Eden Option: Choosing a Story 1 Life in a Story 2 World*

"Reading Betsy St. Amant Haddox is like having coffee with a friend who isn't afraid to tell it like it is. She takes us from the end of her marriage to the other side, and she does so buoyed with hope, compassion, and wisdom for anyone walking that same road."

Micha Boyett, host of *The Slow Way* and author of *Found: A Story of Questions, Grace, and Everyday Prayer*

"*Once Upon a Divorce* offers the healing many women are looking for through heart, humor, and the Holy Spirit. St. Amant Haddox's poignant authenticity is relatable and sure to inspire readers."

Angela Ruth Strong, award-winning author of *Husband Auditions*

"What a gem this book is. Betsy takes us into the deep end to tread water and experience the raw waves of divorce. She encourages us to swim for a while rather than rushing to dry ground. She's not afraid to admit her doubts, fears, and mistakes while offering hope that can only come from an authentic, grounded relationship with Jesus Christ. There's no separating God from our everyday experiences, and Betsy makes that clear—without Jesus, we can do nothing. Through grace-filled advice and wisdom, Betsy helps readers remember their source of hope so they can lean wholly on the Father for comfort and recovery in his timing."

Tez Brooks, author of the award-winning *The Single Dad Detour: Directions for Fathering After Divorce*

Once Upon a Divorce

Walking With God After "The End"

BETSY ST. AMANT HADDOX

KREGEL
PUBLICATIONS

Cataloging-in-Publication data is available from the Library of Congress.

ISBN 978-0-8254-4798-3, print
ISBN 978-0-8254-7075-2, epub
ISBN 978-0-8254-6975-6, Kindle

Printed in the United States of America
24 25 26 27 28 29 30 31 32 33 / 5 4 3 2 1

To my tribe, who walked me through my darkest season—thank you for shining the light of Christ at my feet so I may hold the flashlight now for others. You know who you are.

Now to him who is able to do far more abundantly than all that we ask or think, according to the power at work within us, to him be glory in the church and in Christ Jesus throughout all generations, forever and ever. Amen.

Ephesians 3:20–21

Contents

CONTENTS

We Never Wanted to Be Here

I NEVER WANTED TO WRITE this book.

In fact, when I was going through my divorce years ago, people would tell me well-meaning things like, "You're going to have such a testimony one day." I know they were trying to be encouraging, but it just made me angry. I didn't want a testimony—I wanted my marriage back. I wanted my normal. I wanted the ground to stop shaking under me. I wanted security.

People who had been through divorce themselves would think they were helping when they'd tell me they were "proof from the other side" and that there was "hope from the other side." But all I could see was the gaping chasm between us, and I had no desire to get there. I wanted to go back to the side I knew, dysfunctional as it was.

Like it or not, I was pushed over the edge.

If you're reading this, you can likely relate. Perhaps right now you're in the middle of your own separation or divorce and feel like you're free-falling with no end in sight. Experiencing a constant rush of emotions, fear screaming the loudest, and you just want solid ground again. I remember.

Regardless of the circumstances or specifics, divorce is a chaotic, messy experience.

I grew up in a culture where divorce was not only messy but a major stigma. A permanent scarlet letter, a tattoo, a brand on your heart that would never quite rub off. Despite ministry and outreach and every attempt at reconciliation—divorce simply stained and lingered.

Because of that negative perception, I had no idea how to handle it when the shadow of divorce engulfed my own life. I didn't want it, nor was I willing. Yet without my having a single choice or say in the matter, it was happening.

I was getting my first tattoo, scarlet red.

But God began moving people into my path who spoke life into me.

Men and women who had been there, who told me important truths about my worth and my value. People who reminded me of God's heart for me, who hugged me and cried with me. Who fought for me and refused to let me fall prey to Satan's tricks and ploys and rebounds, who weren't afraid to get dirty in the trenches with me, who weren't afraid of my blood and tears and permanently mascara-streaked face. Who weren't afraid to listen to me vent the same tired plethora of fears and doubts and regrets one more time.

Men and women who prayed over me, with me, and for me when I couldn't find the will to do it for myself anymore. True heroes of the faith, armed with the Word of God, frosty cans of Coke, Starbucks cups, Chex Mix (long story), and gift cards—fighting a war on my behalf when I was too exhausted to even raise my face from the mud.

So many people told me so many helpful things. (And plenty of unhelpful things too—that's a different chapter!)

But there's one thing that no one told me, and I'm going to whisper it to you now. There's a crucial factor to surviving this journey that once seemed so long, so endless, and so very dark. One fact you can embrace, regardless of how far along you are in the process.

Are you ready?

It's okay.

Not it's *going* to be okay—which you have already heard and don't believe—but rather it *is* okay. *Right now.* Exactly where you are, ex-actly what you feel—in this moment, right this second—it's okay.

Let that sink in.

"Going to be okay" and "it is okay" contain such a stark difference. The first statement is true, but it implies that it will be okay someday *if* you don't mess it up. But the second statement reminds you that you don't have to strive. You don't have to pretend and keep redoing your makeup and investing in waterproof mascara. You don't have to put on the charade of "good Christian woman" and act as if you have all the answers.

> **Exactly where you are, exactly what you feel—in this moment, right this second— it's okay.**

You aren't going to walk this perfectly, so right now, wherever you are—you're okay.

Take a deep breath with me, and let that sink in. You're okay. It doesn't feel like that's true, because nothing about your *circumstances* is okay. It's so hard to see beyond what we're currently in the middle of, but the entire horizon is out there, and it's bright. Consider me your silhouette on that horizon, beckoning you over as living proof that more exists. God exists. And while your pain also very much exists, it's not the end of the story. God is a faithful author, and he's already written your next chapter. There is much to hope for.

Like I said, I never wanted to write this book, and I almost didn't. My thought early on was, "People get divorced every day. My story isn't really that dramatic. I was never held at gunpoint and there was no earthquake or celebrity involved. There's nothing uniquely special about my situation that merits an entire book . . . so why should I write it?"

But then I realized that was exactly why I needed to write it. Because a lot of my regular, everyday story is your story too. And if I want you to take anything away from this book, it's that you are seen. In that seeing, I hope to pass to you, through these tear-stained pages, the hope I discovered that can also be yours.

If going through a divorce is your current situation, then I would wager that right now, you're one of two women:

1. The one with the fiery look in her eyes and stubborn tilt to her chin, who wears those high heels even though they pinch a little too tight, because your heart is valiantly thrumming for validation. Because you feel like if you can stand a little taller, you'll get *it* back. You aren't entirely sure what *it* is, but you lost it, and now you need it.

2. The woman who slinks to the back of the crowd because you can't stand the attention. Your eyes stay downcast because you're desperately searching for *it* as you dodge the gossip and the pitying stares. You don't want another casserole or to be put on a prayer request list. You want *it* back.

I've been both of those women. And I know what *it* is.

It's your story.

Hear this, dear sister. The victory of overcoming divorce isn't found in rushing back down the aisle. It's not found via winning in court or obtaining full custody or buying a bigger house than your ex. It's not found in rejoicing in your ex's inevitable pitfalls and woes. It's not found in revenge, a hot date, or a new pair of heels. True victory lies in accepting and then telling your testimony—your beautiful, unique, messy, chaotic story—to the glory of God.

You still have *it*, and it's far from over.

Chapter 1

When Dry Bones Breathe
(and What to Do When They Don't)

MY HUSBAND OF NINE YEARS left me on a cold night in February. He'd just attended a Christian men's retreat on the West Coast that was meant to help him find himself, find the Lord, find everything he thought he was missing. Heart pounding, anxious to hear the results of the trip and what it meant for our marriage, I picked him up from the airport, drove him through Wendy's for a late dinner— and then watched him trade clothes out of his suitcase. This time, the trip wouldn't be to California for six days of worship, treetop obstacle courses, and spiritual healing. This time, the destination was only a few miles down the road to a single friend's house for an undetermined duration.

I'd known this was potentially coming for over a year. But even if you've spent more than 365 days living in the paralyzing anticipation of your worst fear, it's something altogether different when that which you dreaded finally arrives . . . when that specific storm actually sweeps through the front door of your double-wide trailer and takes your husband and everything you've ever known in your adult life with it.

While he packed, I collapsed on the kitchen floor, the faux tiles cold on my knees, listening to my heartbeat pulse an erratic rhythm in my ears. I couldn't breathe. There was no oxygen. But there *was* the name of Jesus, and somehow, despite being physically unable to suck in air, I could breathe out his name. Despite my world crashing black and frigid around me, despite the shadow of despair clouding my home, there was the unmistakable presence of Christ.

It was me and him, and he became the oxygen I could breathe.

Holy ground isn't only found in temples and burning bushes. Sometimes it's discovered right in the middle of north Louisiana on the vented floor of a mobile home.

> **Despite the shadow of despair clouding my home, there was the unmistakable presence of Christ.**

My husband left with a duffel bag and a stony expression. I was left with the task of comforting our four-year-old daughter who didn't understand why Daddy was leaving again.

"You just got home," she wailed.

I felt like crying out the same. But while it takes two to get married, it only takes one to get divorced.

You've been there. Oh sure, your specifics vary—kids or no kids, February nights or June mornings. Maybe your last meal together was a grilled steak instead of Wendy's chicken nuggets. But if you've been abandoned by a spouse, you know that feeling on the floor. Perhaps your floor was carpet or wood or only a figurative floor in your heart. But it absorbed your tears just the same.

Divorce pain is unbearably unique. It's similar to the pain of losing a spouse to death, except in most cases, the grief-stricken widow isn't haunted by waves of betrayal. In most cases, the spouse who passes away didn't directly choose to leave. With divorce, the grief of losing a marriage and a life together—and the person you love dearly—is thrust upon you, *as well as* the anger of rejection. Coat all of that with the sticky, lingering hope that maybe it's not over, and you have the perfect storm for a toxic behavior pattern to manifest. No wonder processing a divorce is messy. It's so multifaceted, it's hard to even know where to begin.

I think that's why many women like you and me simply don't ever start processing it at all. Who has the time? We put on a brave front for the kids, buy a few things to mask the pain, maybe turn to various mild addictions, and soldier on. We take the country song lyric advice to repair our makeup and shake off the breakup.

But denying the need to heal doesn't eliminate the diagnosis or the prognosis. Surgery is required to fix what's wrong, not a quick, DIY patch-up job. If you attempt to fix yourself with the equivalent of a first aid kit, eventually, you're going to run out of Band-Aids. When you do, you'll find you still have a gaping wound. Trust me, I tried it all until the Lord got me on the proverbial surgical table and granted me healing.

I've heard divorce compared to trying to separate two pieces of paper that were glued together—it's impossible to do cleanly. There will be holes and fragments left on both sides after the pieces have been ripped apart because, at one point, they were one. "For this reason a man shall leave his father and his mother, and be joined to his wife; and they shall become one flesh" (Genesis 2:24 NASB).

What do you do when you don't want to rip your papers apart, but you're not given a choice? What then?

I certainly didn't know what to do except pray, and I did that with all my heart. I knew the issue wasn't just the dynamics of our naive young marriage, it was also a spiritual battle warring for my husband. He was wounded, had been through a measure of pain and grief, and was at a crossroads: turn to the Lord or sprint the other direction. I had hoped his heart would be restored on that spiritual retreat, but since it wasn't, I was going to keep praying until it happened. Logic told me that we as a couple couldn't be healed until *he* was healed.

Since he left so abruptly, my husband didn't take all his belongings with him. He packed work clothes and enough basics for a week or two and hit the road to his friend's house, leaving behind most of his closet's contents.

So I gathered an entire outfit—jeans, belt, socks, and shoes. Boxers. A long-sleeve shirt. A hat. I laid it all on the bed accordingly so it looked as if he'd been in the clothes and suddenly vanished right out of them. At the time, that's exactly like what I felt had happened.

Then I grabbed my Bible, took a deep breath, and began praying Ezekiel 37:1–6 out loud:

> The hand of the LORD was upon me, and he brought me out in the Spirit of the LORD and set me down in the middle of the valley; it was full of bones. And he led me around among them, and behold, there were very many on the surface of the valley, and behold, they were very dry. And he said to me, "Son of man, can these bones live?" And I answered, "O Lord GOD, you know." Then he said to me, "Prophesy over these bones, and say to them, O dry bones, hear the word of the LORD. Thus says the Lord GOD to these bones: Behold, I will cause breath to enter you, and you shall live. And I will lay sinews upon you, and will cause flesh to come upon you, and cover you with skin, and put breath in you, and you shall live, and you shall know that I am the LORD."

I prayed for who knows how long, swinging the Sword of the Spirit with all my might, begging for God to breathe life back into my husband so he could find what he was missing.

If you couldn't tell by now, it was important to me that I try everything—literally, everything—to save my marriage. If there had been an award for "most determined to win her husband back," I'd have a shelf of trophies.

At the time, I thought if I could somehow find the right formula, the right words to pray, the right heart posture, the right mix of all these things, then *boom*—it would happen. Heart change complete, marriage restored.

While deep down I knew there was no magic formula, I desperately clung to the belief that I could somehow make it happen. Me.

Welcome to Control Freaks Anonymous, y'all. I'll be your president.

I could look back at that night and roll my eyes at my naivete. I could be bitter and proclaim that the Lord just doesn't answer prayer. Or I could dust off my shoulder with pride and say, "Well, I tried. It wasn't my fault."

But I look back at that night, and I only see the Holy Spirit lovingly directing my steps, blessing me and my obedience to follow the prompting of my terrified, vulnerable heart. I believe the Lord loved that faith offering I raised up. And I think God gave me the idea of breathing life into dry bones, not for my husband but for me. I was gasping for air too and didn't even know it.

Just like God met me on the floor in the kitchen when I couldn't breathe, he met me in my bedroom, right there in front of a pile of country-boy clothing, and reminded me he would be my breath. Coming back to life wasn't going to happen by my own effort.

After that night, there would still be months of gritting my teeth and clenching my fists and trying my hardest before true surrender occurred, but that wild gesture with my husband's clothes became my first step toward true freedom. Like he has continued to do throughout my journey of divorce, God took me down the path of darkness until a glimmer of light began to shine at the far end. Brighter and brighter, each step of the way, each breath along the way, until I was free. What

I thought would be prayer and processing and healing for my husband turned into processing and healing for *me*.

This can be your story too. Right now, that vise around your heart grips tight, squeezing out all hope and cutting off your breath and vision of the good God still has for you. He *does* have good . . . and he is good. And you know what else? He stays that way, whether marriages are restored or not. Sometimes they are, and it's beautiful. I know a young woman who, after divorcing and marrying another man, ended up years later divorced again. She remarried her first husband, and then they had another baby together! That's a powerful testimony.

But not all marriages are resurrected. Not everyone has a Lazarus story, no matter how hard they pray. Trust me, there are plenty of scammers out there who promise if you pay their fee and join their club, your spouse will come trotting right back to you. Take twenty seconds to google (actually, please don't), and you'll find a plethora of articles with tips on how to manipulate and trick your man into wanting you back. There is even witchcraft out there that offers to hocus-pocus your husband right home. I'm sure you've seen them in your spam folders or as spam posts on blogs.

> **Not all marriages are resurrected. Not everyone has a Lazarus story, no matter how hard they pray.**

Please don't waste time or a single penny on any of that madness. It's ridiculous. No human can promise anything on behalf of another. You don't need worldly tricks and pagan rituals when you have access via prayer to the very One who created your husband in the first place. God knows him best, and only he knows what is truly needed.

I understand the desperation you feel. You want to be free at all costs. You want the pain and hurt to stop—*now*. But it's a process, and despite the thrum of lies telling you otherwise, you're not desperate.

You can pour all that heartache and energy and pleading into prayer to your heavenly Father. Pray for your spouse—and pray for yourself. You don't know what the Lord might do in your husband's heart, but I absolutely know what he can do in yours.

Your marriage might not be a Lazarus story, but your oxygen-starved heart absolutely can be resurrected.

Chapter 2

Just When You Think You Have God Figured Out

REMEMBER WHEN I SAID I tried everything to get my husband back? I really did, including gathering my entire family, multiple friends, and church members at my parents' house for intercessory prayer one night. I hadn't fully given up on the concept of being able to pray my spouse back home, despite the niggling thought that it wasn't exactly working. I became convinced I could see where the story was going, and that I had the inside scoop.

Spoiler alert—I didn't. In fact, I was so far off, I couldn't have scooped if I'd been handed a shovel.

But the well-meaning comments that night from those gathered in prayer fed my hopes. So many godly men and women I appreciated and loved dearly believed that my husband was coming back. Many of us felt that the prayer night was working. Everyone could feel it. After all, according to Matthew 18:19–20, we had the boxes checked.

We were in agreement. Check.

There were more than two or three of us. Check, check.

And we were praying and asking in Jesus's name, so bonus, we also had John 14:13 covered.[1] Check.

Unfortunately, my theology at the time was a little off. I've since learned Scripture can't be wielded to manipulate God or be chanted like a magic formula. My prayers at that time sounded more like I was attempting to force God into a corner. "Your Word says this, and I'm praying it, so you have to do what I want—right?"

I told you divorce was messy.

I read the Bible and multiple articles and devotionals, thinking they would help me predict what God was going to do in my marriage. If I read an article about a woman whose marriage was restored, I had hope. If I read about one that God never repaired, I scrolled past it with a sinking heart. I became consumed with resources, each one seemingly a premonition or sign that my marriage would follow in the same path. It was exhausting. I read Scripture the same way and thought, "God is obviously against divorce. So that means he will do a miracle here and put us back together."

I also found these alleged signs in my circumstances. For example: As a fiction author, I was used to my agent sending out my book proposals to various publishers over the years. I'd had eight novels published with Harlequin Love Inspired at the time and was attempting to break into a publishing house that allowed longer stories. Then a few weeks after my ex walked out the door, I got the call.

A two-book deal from my dream publisher.

It's hard to celebrate with a broken heart, but I sure tried. My family took me, my daughter, and a good friend of mine to dinner at a local bistro, where I signed the paper contract from my new publisher and ate French food and ordered a lot of dessert. I look back on those pictures now and notice how fake my smile was (and my hair color, for that matter!) and immediately remember the rush of feelings washing over me that night. I could list them all, but the overwhelming sensation was simply that it wasn't supposed to be this way. The empty chair at the table felt glaringly obvious. I had finally done it. The big contract had finally come, and my husband wasn't there to celebrate.

I felt robbed. And it made me angry—it was just one more thing he had ruined.

That contract also gave me false hope. I discussed with my mother that surely this book deal meant my husband would come back. *Surely* God didn't expect me to write romance when my own love life was gasping for air.

But that's exactly what God expected me to do.

And the good news is, he didn't leave me to do it alone. It turns out, God answers prayers—even the ones where we don't fully understand what we're asking for. I have a vivid memory of drying my hair in my bathroom a few months before my ex left. I remember staring at the counter and feeling so out of sorts. I had no idea what was coming, but my heart knew *something* was coming. A feeling of impending change was there and tangible. A wordless prayer for God to go with me was on my heart, despite not even knowing I needed to pray.

> **God answers prayers—even the ones where we don't fully understand what we're asking for.**

There was another time, the fall before my husband left, where I was at the annual writers' conference I look forward to each September. I was sitting in the worship time, immersed in the music and the presence of the Holy Spirit, and I remember thinking how badly I wanted to go deeper. How I wanted to infuse my novels with more meaning, emotion, and depth. I had no idea how to do it. But God did. He answered that prayer of my heart, even though he used incredibly difficult circumstances to get me there.

Please hear me. I'm not saying every bad feeling we get comes true. And I'm certainly not saying God decided to break up my marriage to help me write better fiction. But I *am* saying he prepares our hearts. He knows what we need before we need it, and he often begins to equip us and steer us in that direction before we're even aware enough to recognize it.

Told you he was good.

Without my divorce, I never would have realized how shallow my faith was. When I share my testimony, I always point out how before my divorce, I had never needed God. Oh sure, I prayed to receive salvation as a child and walked the orange-carpeted aisle at church the following Sunday to make it official with the pastor. I got baptized, then spent several years as a perfectionistic, people-pleasing child fighting anxiety that I hadn't done it right. That somehow, I had prayed the wrong thing and my salvation wasn't entirely secure, and so I kept praying. Sometimes, that prayer was like reciting a mantra over and over while riding in the back seat of my mom's car. As a teenager I got baptized again, hoping I could put to rest the doubts and have another tangible mile marker to reflect upon.

As an adult who has overcome a lot of anxiety and OCD tendencies, I realize now that the faith I had as a seven-year-old was genuine. I understood salvation. I knew the cross. I fully absorbed what Jesus did and how I was hopeless without him because, even as a good girl, I was a wretched sinner.

But the faith I had as a child that meant so much to me could only carry me for so long. The Bible points out that we shouldn't live on spiritual milk indefinitely (Hebrews 5:11–14). And my faith was about to get a big ol' piece of steak. Our salvation is never at risk—but our doctrine sure is. The night my husband walked out the door, I came to an impasse in my faith. I felt like there were only two options: one, to believe that God was sovereign and in control and therefore would put my marriage back together, or two, that God wasn't in control, and this was all up to my spouse, and therefore reconciliation might not happen.

At the time, I couldn't see the truth—which was that both of those things were true. God is sovereign and in control, *and* my husband had the ability to make choices that negatively affected me.

All the carefully crafted formulas I had subconsciously created over my twenty-nine years of life tumbled around me:

- Bad things only happened to people who weren't living right. Nothing bad would happen to me because I was a good girl.
- If I didn't cuss and had a regular quiet time and faithfully attended church, I wouldn't ever have to go through anything hard.
- God and I had a deal—I laid low and tried my hardest to be good, and he would work things out for me.

Does this resonate? Think about it. Where is your faith right now? Are you stumbling around in the dark, stubbing your toe on the facts that are getting in the way of your theology? Maybe, instead of believing in a false "good girl" deal, you believe that you've done too many bad things for God to love you. Or you believe that you're being punished with this divorce because you abused substances or slept around before you got married. Maybe your theology is floundering, as mine did, because it wasn't all that solid to begin with. Does what is happening in your life and your marriage make sense to you, or are you struggling to reconcile it with what you knew—or thought you knew—about the Lord?

When everything else around us is shaken and outside of our control, it can be unbearable to take a hit to our faith too. We need that lifeline more than ever. That's why it's so important to go to God with your questions. When life doesn't make sense, don't withdraw. Instead, press in. Ask. Holler at God. After all, if David (who Scripture says was a man after God's own heart) wrote psalm after psalm of lament and complaints, and vented his grief and anger and fear before the Lord, why can't we? You might not be like David, hiding in a literal cave from an enemy who wants to kill you, but you might be hiding in an emotional cave of despair. On top of that, the Bible is clear that we have an enemy who wants to kill us and steal from us and ultimately destroy us (John 10:10). Don't believe the lie that God is mad at you for feeling confused. Don't think for a minute that God can't handle your questions or that you're a bad Christian for having them. It's normal. Look at David. Look at Job, and even Thomas. The poor guy had to go through all of history with the nickname "Doubting Thomas," but I admire him for being real. He said outright what some of the other disciples were quite possibly thinking. Even if they weren't, Thomas didn't let expectation or fear of judgment hinder his vulnerability.

And the Lord met Thomas and gave him what he needed.

> **Don't believe the lie that God is mad at you for feeling confused.**

He'll do that for you, too, just like he did for me. So don't retreat. Go to him with what doesn't make sense. Flip your Bible open to roughly the middle portion and start reading the Psalms out loud. Lament with David. Cry before the Lord. Express your doubt and confusion and fear over your life not lining up with your faith the way you'd always assumed. Then pray and ask the Holy Spirit to lead you into truth. He is truth, after all (John 14:6).

For me, amid the smoldering ash and settling dust of those false gospels, I found the firm foundation—Christ alone. I finally found my need for him. Not just for my salvation, but for my very next breath. To get out of bed. To put one foot forward and then the next and live as a single mom with a broken heart.

God isn't our lucky charm or our insurance plan—he is our life source. I thought I'd been living just fine with stale air and damaged lungs. Knowing him on a deeper level was the oxygen I'd been craving all along and didn't even realize I needed. I thought I had God and the Christian life all figured out.

And because he is so, so good, he showed me that I didn't.

Chapter 3

When You Don't Want to Pray

DURING MY SEASON OF DIVORCE, I swung from hosting prayer meetings in my parents' home and essentially bossing God around in prayer to not wanting to pray at all. That's what happens when we feel rejected. We pull back.

My prayers didn't appear to be working in the way I wanted, despite my systematic walk through the incredibly encouraging book *The Power of a Praying Wife* by Stormie Omartian and my regular consumption of devotionals, podcasts, and articles on marriage. I read John and Stasi Eldredge's *Love & War* every night for a week in a hot bubble bath, seeking answers and advice until the water ran cold and I was forced to go back to my incredibly lukewarm reality.

When I was reading that kind of material, I felt so fired up. It seemed like miracles were only a breath away—a prayer away. Yet when I prayed, nothing happened.

I wasn't sure what to make of that, and I didn't want to make God mad, so I tried to hide my frustrated feelings. You can imagine how effective that was!

Somehow we believe if we can just keep it together long enough, things will go the way we hope. Like maybe God will forget the good work he is completing in me and leave me to my own devices with a restored marriage and my familiar, albeit toxic, sense of normal.

You know the feeling I'm talking about, don't you? It's ultimately an attempted grasp for control. We technically have no control of our circumstances, but we think if we can maneuver things just right or find the right formula with prayer and petition or attend enough church services in a single week, then we can at least pretend we have control.

But we never will. Look around you. People who seem to be the holiest ones you know struggle with divorce, disease, wayward children, infertility, and financial burdens, while criminals and atheists easily thrive, conceive, and have good relationships. Matthew 5:45 sums it up well: "For he makes his sun rise on the evil and on the good, and sends rain on the just and on the unjust."

There is no formula, friend. You're not going to earn God's favor or answered prayers by attending church more often or stuffing down your hurt or anger when you pray. His presence in your life is not contingent on whether you successfully bit back that last cuss word or drank one beer or two. If you're a believer, God's Spirit is with you, period.

And he is not judging you or withholding blessing because you're not handling this crisis of faith perfectly.

Maybe you weren't the one who was left. Maybe you had to do the leaving, but the circumstances surrounding that choice felt as much out of your control as if you'd been abandoned. Or perhaps you fought the Lord for a formula of your own—if you did this or that, your spouse would change, the abuse would stop, the criminal record would clear, the substance abuse would end, or the unrepentant adultery would cease.

Maybe you sat around for months or even years with a racing heart and adrenaline-flooded veins as your formula failed, waiting as long as you could before making the hard decision to open the front door and step into the unknown.

If that's you, I'm so sorry. You're facing a slightly different but just as difficult path—maybe one laden with even more judgment from outsiders who don't know the full situation. May I encourage you with the truth that God sees? He knows the details. He understands the havoc wreaked in your heart. And he is not tattooing you with any scarlet letter. Don't stop praying. Don't stop being honest with him. He's not rejecting you.

> **God is not judging you or withholding blessing because you're not handling this crisis of faith perfectly.**

As an author, I'm very familiar with rejection. I'm used to getting "no thanks" responses from editors regarding new fiction projects. It's not unusual for my agent to email me, "Sorry, they passed on it," regarding a new proposal I'd hoped to contract into a book deal. Rejection is part of being an author. After all, not every proposal makes it to the bookshelf. When those emails come, we simply start over. We go back to the drawing board (or in this case, the blinking cursor) and begin a new project. Eventually, we find one that is a good fit, and there's much rejoicing in the land when the contract is signed. (We call it Snoopy dancing!)

While I already knew rejection professionally and was becoming all too familiar with rejection personally from my ex, I was not prepared to handle feeling rejected spiritually. What do you do when your life is falling apart and your prayers seem to bounce off the ceiling?

To make matters worse, when I sought encouragement from others, I often got advice I didn't want to hear. Thankfully, while my marriage had not survived the "for better or for worse" vow, the "worse" in this case turned out to be for the better.

One of my dear friends in my writing community, Angela, had walked through an unwanted divorce not long ahead of me. She was lovely and fierce and had just gotten remarried to a wonderful godly man who adored her. She was the epitome of beauty from ashes. I remember going to her for advice, eager for her assurance that the same would happen to me.

But because she was a true friend, she didn't offer what I wanted. How could she give me what she wasn't sure of? She couldn't see the future. Of course she had no idea if my ex would come back or if I'd ever find another spouse.

Instead, Angela offered me what she was certain of—Scripture and prayer. Every time I messaged or emailed seeking some form of earthly "this will all work out for you, don't worry," I got a Bible verse. Or I received sympathy and encouragement, but it was always via Bible verses, prayer, and the reminder that I was seen and not alone. I don't think she ever once told me I would get remarried, though she might have thought it entirely possible. Instead, she stuck to what she knew I needed—the truth. And in the midst of a divorce, Jesus is the only way, truth, and life (John 14:6).

In the same vein, one of the things I heard most frequently from well-meaning friends was that I would one day be able to comfort with the comfort I had been given, à la 2 Corinthians 1:3–4: "Blessed be the God and Father of our Lord Jesus Christ, the Father of mercies and God of all comfort, who comforts us in all our affliction, so that we may be able to comfort those who are in any affliction, with the comfort with which we ourselves are comforted by God."

> In the midst of a divorce, Jesus is the only way, truth, and life.

I felt like I had even Paul beat as "the chief of sinners" when I admitted I didn't want that. I didn't want to make other people feel better in some elusive future—I wanted to feel better right then. I didn't want to go through something hard just to make someone else's struggle easier down the road. Honestly, at the time, that felt ludicrous to even ask of me. I couldn't begin to see a life on the other side of this storm—all I saw was darkness and swirling clouds of debris. The sunshine felt permanently banished.

I was definitely *not* okay.

And I later realized something priceless—it's okay not to be okay.

I love the story of Moses in Exodus 17. Joshua was leading a battle to fight Amalek, and it was Moses's job to stand on the hill with his staff. Whenever Moses held up his hand, Israel prevailed against their enemy. But when he lowered his hand, the enemy gained ground. Despite the miracle of such an event, Moses's arms grew weary. Eventually, he sat on a giant stone while Aaron and Hur held up his hands for him.

Sit with that for a moment.

There are times when we know what to do but simply can't muster the energy to do so. Even when our faith is strong and the miracle is near, it's okay to let others lift our hands for a season. It doesn't make any of us a failure. Would you call Moses a failure? Of course not! But if even Moses needed assistance, how much more do we need to be lifted up by our fellow believers? That's why when you feel like you can't pray, you seek out the prayers of others.

If you don't have a group of trusted advisers and friends willing to tell you hard truths and hold your arms up in prayer while you avoid even looking into the heavens, I encourage you to find them immediately. I look back on my journey and have no idea what I would have done without my community supporting me.

Here's the catch—to get them, you must be vulnerable.

You might be reeling back right now or tempted to throw this book across the room. I get it. It's easier to eat ice cream out of the tub alone, but trust me—you don't want to miss this step. Grab more spoons and find your squad. Get real about your feelings, your needs, and your struggle to other women in your church (same-gender support is crucial) and simply ask. You might be surprised at how many responses you get from people eager to love on you.

And if there are those in your life who can't lift you up, if they find your struggles too burdensome because of what they're already carrying, they weren't meant to be on your team. Someone out there is, and they've been equipped by the Lord to meet you in your need. (More on that later!)

For now, in this spiritually dry season, you need to give yourself grace. A divorce isn't the time to attempt to be Super Christian. The cape will only choke you. It's okay to turn on worship music and lie face down on the carpet when completely unable to sing. It's okay to try to pray but only cry instead. It's okay to turn on a podcast about Christian marriage and end up covering your ears. You're in grief. You're mourning the death of a relationship and your dreams. And whether reconciliation ever follows or not, you've got to allow yourself to go through the various steps of grief right where you are. You can't skip them—you'll do more harm than good.

If you're anything like me, you might feel guilty in this dry stage and catch yourself thinking things like:

- If I don't handle this well, God won't put my marriage back together.
- If I sin at all during this season, I'll lose my chance to have restoration.
- If I don't walk this perfectly, I'll for sure not get what I want.

I have one word for that—poppycock.

God didn't remain seemingly silent during that early season in my divorce because I was hurting or angry or confused. And he's not doing that to you either. He was sitting with me in my pain, offering his healing presence in ways I couldn't see until much later. He never expected perfection from me—and he doesn't expect it from you.

Think about it this way. If you broke your leg, would anyone begrudge you your inability to walk? That you need help navigating on crutches, opening doors, and doing basic things for yourself like showering or cooking or getting the mail? Do you think the Lord would judge you for needing pain medication or not being able to make it to church for a few weeks? Of course not—that'd be silly.

If you're walking through a divorce, odds are, you've got a broken heart. You need help from others to navigate this new life you're in. You need assistance doing basic things for yourself in your season of grief. And God isn't begrudging your pain or judging you for needing time to wallow. He will meet you in that hurt, wrap you up, and send you special blessings from himself—but you won't see them if you're not purposefully looking for them.

One evening I was lying in bed unable to sleep but lacking the desire to be anywhere else. I briefly found the gumption to pray, but it quickly waned. The tears came back, and between prayer attempts and gut-wrenching sobs, I couldn't breathe. Just like that night when my ex first left, I found myself on the floor of my double-wide, unable to breathe or say anything other than the name of Jesus. And you know what? He was enough. He was my breath. It was the oddest sensation, feeling as if I were breathing without the mechanical act of drawing breath into my lungs. But for those few minutes, it happened.

He is our breath. He is our life source.

We aren't doing this alone.

Romans 8:26 says, "Likewise the Spirit helps us in our weakness. For we do not know what to pray for as we ought, but the Spirit himself intercedes for us with groanings too deep for words."

Later in that same book, Paul wrote, in verse 34, "Christ Jesus is the one who died—more than that, who was raised—who is at the right hand of God, who indeed is interceding for us."

We have an intercessor in Christ. What amazing news! Jesus literally prays for us, even when our faith is weak. Even when we can't push words off our lips or draw breath into our weary bodies. Even when we're hurt and angry and confused. Even when our faith feels wobbly. He doesn't abandon us to our pain.

Not even when we don't want to pray.

So when your prayers are bouncing off the ceiling or you can't seem to muster any words in the first place, it's okay. It doesn't mean you're a failure of a Christian. It means you're normal. Don't worry—the desire to pray will eventually return. For today, all you need to do is bask in the realization that Jesus is praying for you instead.

Amen.

Chapter 4

Spongy Dinosaurs & Unlikely Blessings

I'M TRULY AMAZED HOW MANY blessings were sent my way during the worst season of my life. While I never want to live those days again, the silver lining to my dark thundercloud shone gloriously bright. Funny how we can smile when looking back on things we thought we'd never survive.

The faint glow of a silver lining might have started with my boss at the part-time job I'd acquired in the months before my ex left me. I worked a few days a week, sitting in that little country water department office, managing accounts and making calls to remind people their bills were due. I got yelled at a lot by folks who didn't want to be told their water was getting shut off for nonpayment, but my co-workers were great. And when my husband left and we were officially separated, they were there, offering smiles and hugs and pretending not to notice my persistently bloodshot eyes or the worship songs I blared from my desktop computer. They brought me cold cans of soda, reminded me how amazing I was, and told me silly stories to make me laugh. I'll never forget their kindness.

One day I started driving to work, pulled over on the side of the road, and called my boss to tell him I couldn't stop crying long enough to come in. He responded with sympathy and understanding, something I will also never forget, and I went back home—with pay. Eventually, my job there had to come to an end because I couldn't support myself on a part-time paycheck. But I still remember him with extreme fondness.

Or maybe the silver lining began the time I got pulled over one Sunday for speeding down a country road on my way to drop off my daughter to her dad for her next visit, and the middle-aged sheriff gave this hurting mama a little warning and a whole lot of grace.

Writing this chapter, I relate strongly to the verses of Hebrews 11:32–34.

> And what more shall I say? For time would fail me to tell of Gideon, Barak, Samson, Jephthah, of David and Samuel and the prophets—who through faith conquered kingdoms, enforced justice, obtained promises, stopped the mouths of lions, quenched the power of fire, escaped the edge of the sword, were made strong out of weakness, became mighty in war, put foreign armies to flight.

Just like for Gideon and the rest of these guys, there were so many blessings, time would fail me to tell of them all. Such as the way I stumbled into an online prayer group that called each other every Tuesday evening to pray for each other's marriages. Total strangers, stretched across the country, praying for restoration and healing for their mutual wounds. I tear up thinking about it even now because it's such a beautiful concept. I especially bonded with one woman named Jennifer. We kept up after the group calls dwindled, and we're still close friends today. In fact, she drove from Florida to Louisiana a few years ago to attend my wedding.

If I hadn't gone through that horrific season, I'd have never experienced any of those gifts.

I bet you can identify. A stranger paid for your coffee that one especially hard morning on the way to work. Or you were given grace in a situation where you normally wouldn't have received it. Perhaps you were given an unexpected hug or gift card or offer for a night out.

I challenge you to write down your blessings. Right now, it might be that you can only see the swirling storm and the pressing darkness, but I promise you, one day you'll want to remember those little moments when the clouds parted and the favor of the Lord shone on you in special, specific ways. They're there, and they're happening—document them. Keep a log or a journal of some sort, even if it's just shooting an email to yourself. Those memories are some of my sweetest.

Leave yourself a trail of bread crumbs to follow back to God's goodness.

Another sweet blessing occurred the week my ex moved out. I went to my parents' house because I couldn't stand to be alone in my grief. I remember lying face down on the carpeted floor in my mom's home office, immersed in grief, when my niece toddled in. She would have been around three years old at the time and clearly didn't understand what had happened or what I was going through. But without saying a word, she handed me a little pink-and-yellow creature she'd created out of Legos, smiled, and ran out of the room. She wanted to cheer up her "Aunt B." I still have it in my dresser drawer.

> **Leave yourself a trail of bread crumbs to follow back to God's goodness.**

I also still have emails and screenshots of text messages from friends building me up and reminding me where my true worth and identity comes from (spoiler alert—not from my ex). I still have vivid memories of arms wrapping me tight at a writers' conference, where the deepest friends of my heart rallied around me. I remember all the offers to mow my yard or babysit and the invitations to hang out so I wouldn't be alone.

There are blessings.

But I get it. Some weeks, the nights stretch long and the only blessing you can see from your tear-soaked pillow is the fact that at least when you fall asleep, you won't be hurting for roughly seven hours. Some days, just plodding from the carpool line to your day job to cooking dinner is harder than walking with lead weights tied to your shoes. Those days, maybe the only blessing you can conjure up is that the sun feels good on your face when you trudge to get the mail. But it's a start.

Sometimes the blessings seem small. They remind me of those toys my daughter used to beg me to buy every time we saw one—tiny spongy dinosaurs or spaceships that you immerse in water and that, after several hours, are suddenly enormous! In that same way, the more you acknowledge your blessings, the bigger they grow. The more you saturate your mind and heart and thoughts with the goodness of God (even when it feels like a stretch), the bigger your blessings will appear to you.

You might be thinking, "I don't deserve any blessings," because you were the one who had to make the impossible decision to leave for your safety or well-being or that of your children, and you feel guilty. Or maybe you didn't ask for the divorce or the separation, but you feel responsible for your part in what went wrong. You have thoughts such as, "If only I had done this," "If only I had said that," or "If only I'd done better in this area, I would still be married."

That's normal.

It's also completely untrue. The only person you can control in a marriage is yourself. Any wondering about what you could have done differently to get different circumstances is pure speculation and will drive you crazy. You have no idea if things would have changed if you'd only done such and such. Things just as likely could have gotten worse. I compromised on a *lot* that last year of my marriage, attempting to convince my ex to stay. Needless to say, it didn't work.

So don't go down that road. Don't pull back and try to convince yourself you deserve what you get now because you somehow weren't perfect along the way. And don't think you're doing yourself or God a favor by pulling away from his comfort.

Think about it like this. If you're a parent, consider your heart toward your children when they mess up or make a bad decision. Do you shun them when they come to you, crying and broken? Or do you bandage their wounds, offer a hug, and gently guide them into a better decision next time? At that point, don't you usually dig out the Popsicles or turn on their favorite show and snuggle on the couch? Or if they're a teenager, isn't that when you offer to hang out and talk or listen to music and "vibe" together?

How would you feel if they shunned your advances toward reconciliation? If they shrugged out of your hug, rejected the Popsicle, and locked themselves in their room for self-inflicted punishment? What if they skipped out on dinner because they thought they didn't deserve to eat after making a mistake? You would find that ridiculous and unnecessary. It would even hurt your feelings.

James 1:17 says, "Every good gift and every perfect gift is from above, coming down from the Father of lights, with whom there is no variation or shadow due to change."

Our Father gives good gifts—even when we're not perfect. No matter what you contributed to the separation or divorce, you are worthy of receiving blessings from God simply because of who *he* is. In the spiritual sense, we're never good enough to deserve anything on our own merit . . . whether we're in healthy marriages or not.

This doesn't mean there isn't room for conviction and repentance. Of course there is. But don't shun the blessings God is giving you in this dark time, even if it's hard to accept them at first. You won't become more pious by punishing yourself and avoiding comfort and healing. You *will*, however, draw closer to God when you praise him for his provision and receive his gifts with open, humble hands. Remember the spongy dinosaur.

> **You are worthy of receiving blessings from God simply because of who *he* is.**

But maybe that's not your struggle at all. Perhaps you don't feel responsible or guilty for your role in the breakup, but you're struggling to accept blessings from the Lord because you just can't see any. The clouds are too thick and dark, and you're angry. Bitterness has seeped in. You can't find any blessings to be grateful for. The bills are piling up, your friendships are strained, and you feel alone. You are more than likely in the middle of big transitions regarding work, income, and housing. And if you have children, you're at the very least hurting for them and, at worst, dealing with an ex who is trying to pit them against you. What's there to be happy about? Life is pure effort and struggle and despair, and it's too much trouble to even cast your eyes to the clouds to see if there's a silver lining present.

I understand. I dealt with what I considered very unfair situations during my separation, including a court-appointed mediator who gave up on us, a custody arrangement that broke my heart, and a judge who had to court order my ex to pay half of the mortgage he walked away from. I know a woman who went through a divorce and had to steal toilet paper for her kids because her ex drained their bank accounts and they were in a true bind. I could tell story after story of unfair, and you probably have your own.

It's easy to let the anger take over—especially because when we're mad, our anger burns bright enough to hide the sad. That anger is a wonderful, albeit temporary, distraction. But when we let anger flare, it also blinds us to the gifts. Gifts of love and support and hope that sometimes creep up slowly behind us, and at other times careen around the bend so quickly they nearly knock us off our feet with joy. Anger blinds us to the anonymous Starbucks gift card sent via email when money is tight, to the sunrise splotching gold and crimson and burgundy across the sky. It blinds us to the precious sleepy snuggles from our littles at the end of the day, the bag of groceries delivered to our doorstep, and the steady stream of prayer for our family from that sweet woman at church.

If you still don't see any gifts right now, don't give up. Keep your eyes open. Ask God to show up—maybe in seeing your favorite color or bird or whatever has meaning to you. God's blessings are coming—they're always coming. And here's a fact that remains true regardless of whether we receive monetary miracles, whether we have children to distract us from the constant pain and grief, whether we notice the beauty of creation around us—Jesus is our greatest blessing. Take a minute to dwell on the following verses.

> Why are you cast down, O my soul,
>   and why are you in turmoil within me?
> Hope in God; for I shall again praise him,
>   my salvation and my God.
>   (Psalm 43:5)

But whatever gain I had, I counted as loss for the sake of Christ. Indeed, I count everything as loss because of the surpassing worth of knowing Christ Jesus my Lord. For his sake I have suffered the loss of all things and count them as rubbish, in order that I may gain Christ. (Philippians 3:7–8)

Your ex might have stolen your marriage from you. He might have stolen away time with your children, money from your bank account, or some of your favorite possessions from your home. But he can never steal your relationship with Christ. He can never take from you the joy of your salvation, the comforting presence of the Holy Spirit, or the gospel message of hope. Your ex might have left, but God promises he never will (Hebrews 13:5).

When that baseline is what we cling to, the blessings begin to pile up. The silver lining glows brightly. And that spongy dinosaur grows bigger and bigger.

Chapter 5

What to Do When Your Church Doesn't Know What to Do

WALKING INTO CHURCH ALONE AFTER my husband left was like that recurring dream I'd had in sixth grade where I was strolling naked through the halls of school. Except this time, it was real. No, I didn't walk into church without clothes on, but my shame made me feel even more exposed in so many ways.

I loved my church. It was a good, Bible-preaching church. But it was proper, and most dirty laundry never saw the light of day. There wasn't such a thing as scandal there, not in my years attending, and I don't think they knew what to do with me. What *do* you do with a twentysomething woman, her runaway husband, and their five-year-old child? People knew the story or at least thought they did. Others were shocked. My friends were caught in the middle, unaware of the whole story and understandably not wanting to take sides.

Not knowing what to do myself, I clung to hope. My marriage would be restored. My husband would come back home. This would all be a different sort of bad dream than the walking-naked one. After all, even the marital counselor we saw before the big split assured me my ex would never actually leave me and was just bluffing.

But he did, and he wasn't. And everyone was at a loss.

So I soldiered on, attending every service alone—sometimes with my chin raised, sometimes with it tucked tightly against my chest in a sob. I started leading a group of young women through the ever-popular *Power of a Praying Wife* book, meeting on Wednesday nights and praying together for all our spouses, no matter where we were in our various relationships. Those evenings, my hope flared the strongest. I felt united in prayer with my Christian sisters, and I could see past all the gloomy, logical evidence staring me in the face. I could see light.

But then I got word that the church staff would prefer my prayer group not meet on Wednesdays. They wanted all the adults on campus together for the church-wide study on Revelation. I was crushed but obeyed. Then another evening, as I poured out my hopes and fears and gave a staff member's sweet wife an update on my marital situation, her response made me recognize it was time to move to a new community. As I told her how much I hoped for restoration and was praying for a miracle, she said, "Now, honey, why would you want to be with someone who doesn't want to be with you?"

I was taken aback. I know she meant well, and in hindsight, it doesn't shock me nearly as much as it did that night. But back then, I didn't have the years and maturity and wisdom to filter that comment.

Have you received comments indicating that your marriage didn't matter? That you were foolish to keep hoping it could be saved? You might have been told things, even well-intentioned things, that only seemed to prove your greatest fear—that your heartache, tears, and confusion are silly. That you should just move on and give up hope.

If you have, you know how that feels. All the hope, faith, and light I'd been so dependent on left in a whoosh, like a slamming door blowing out the last smoldering ember in a near-dark room. My faith was barely flickering, and I needed to go somewhere for a season and hide. Blend in. Find a church community somewhere people didn't already know the whole story (or at least think they did). There's nothing wrong with moving to a safe place to recover.

So I ran back to my childhood church, the one I'd attended my entire life before leaving with my husband to join his church. It was a big congregation, and I had extended family there and could be hugged but not bugged. I could get there right on time and sit in the back and cry if I needed to. I'd been gone long enough that I was surrounded mostly by strangers and could just soak in the comforting presence of the Lord and his Word. In my heart, I knew this was only a stopping-over point. Where I'd go eventually, I had no idea, but I figured God would tell me.

Turns out, he was working to do exactly that.

I sat in my new-old church the Sunday before Easter, somehow feeling invisible and very much spotlighted all at the same time. Then suddenly, the lights dimmed, and a video played via a projector above. A man's bold and booming voice filled the sanctuary as scenes of storms played out on the screen. Then the crucifixion. Despair. Darkness. Yet one phrase was repeated over and over as the man's deep voice described Good Friday.

It's Friday . . . but Sunday is coming.

God has already addressed the hopelessness divorce brings, the despair we feel in our souls so poignantly that it's almost tangible. That Good Friday video acknowledged my specific swirling storm of grief. And the phrase kept repeating.

It's Friday . . . but Sunday is coming.

> **God has already addressed the hopelessness divorce brings, the despair we feel in our souls.**

My throat knotted. Tears streamed down my face, and I didn't make a single effort to hold them back. Sometimes, hope stings. And I hoped until I felt like I might bleed from the effort. That day, I *knew* the message was for me. I thought it meant my marriage was going to be fixed.

And Sunday was coming indeed . . . but not in the way I'd imagined.

That summer, Katie—one of my best friends in my writing community—came for a visit. She flew from Iowa to Louisiana just to be with me. We went rifle shooting, ate chocolate-covered apples that we snuck inside a movie theater, and went to a thrift shop simply for the purpose of buying old, cheap dishware that we proceeded to throw against the side of the barn on my acreage.

Watching the pieces shatter was wildly therapeutic.

But perhaps the best part of the visit (with my young daughter's makeover of my friend—using brightly colored eye shadow and multiple scrunchies—being toward the top of the list!) was the message Katie scrawled on the back of an offertory envelope when we sat in my church pew together.

The pastor was preaching, the service was clicking right along, and suddenly, she began to scribble Ezekiel 34:16 (NIV): "I will search for the lost and bring back the strays. I will bind up the injured and strengthen the weak."

I looked at her, nodding. As in, "Right, that's my prayer for my husband. Great verse for him!"

She shook her head, eyes serious. "I think it's for you."

> "I will search for the lost and bring back the strays. I will bind up the injured and strengthen the weak."

I just stared back. At the time, I didn't want to hear it. I wanted to take every sign as proof that my husband was coming back. I wanted everything to be about him. Turns out, a lot was about me. Now that envelope that was so hard to read is one of my most treasured possessions. It takes me back to the pew that Easter season. God was at work then, preparing for Sunday all along. Even in the darkness that morning, watching the video play and willing it to mean what I wanted it to mean, God was planting the seeds of hope in my heart to blossom in his perfect timing. He's always working behind the scenes, and rarely is it in the way we imagine it will be.

He's working right now for you too. Whatever your story is, whatever that knot in your throat represents, whatever fear leaves your palms sweaty and your smile fake—he's working in you and for you. It might not look the way you hope. But if it doesn't, it's because it's for a better, stronger, truer, more eternal purpose than you could ever imagine.

Your church might not know what to do with you. But God does, and he knows exactly where you need to be in this transition season. He's moving for you behind the scenes, gently guiding you into the place where you can heal.

Even if you're like me and occasionally don't want to hear the healing messages.

Or maybe your church *does* know what to do—perhaps you belong to a body that has an amazing divorce recovery program or a handful of older, wiser mentors to take you under their wing. I sincerely hope so. But if you're like I was back then and you don't have that—you're still not alone. You're tucked under the wing of your heavenly Father (Psalm 91:4).

I know it seems lonely right now. You feel like someone is shining a flashlight on you with all the flattering glory of a department store dressing room. You feel exposed, with all your greatest flaws on display. May I encourage you not to trust or rest in the security of man, but in the assurance of your identity in Christ? Dare I ask you to resist the temptation to people-please, fake smile, and say, "Fine," when they ask how you are?

You're not obligated to perform, dear reader. So please, sit there in the pew and cry. Drop the facade. Sing worship loudly with tears streaming down your face or sit quietly with your hands clenched as you wrestle in prayer. Do whatever it takes to purge the fears and cling to your Father. The hope he provides is true, living, gospel hope that far exceeds any benefits and pleasures of temporary, earthly relationships. And if where you worship isn't a safe place to do all these things, it's okay to find a new place.

There's so much beauty in vulnerability. Never be embarrassed when you show your true emotions and heart. For example—a few Sundays ago while writing this book, I exited the restroom at church and ran into a sweet woman who had been praying for me while I wrote. She casually asked how the writing was going, and I burst into tears.

Right there in the hallway, leaning against the wall outside the restroom, I expressed my fears and the warfare I'd been experiencing while writing. I shared how I doubted so much of the process but also reveled in how there were just as many moments of assurance and divine wisdom prodding me along. I was a roller coaster of all the feels, and she joined me on the ride as tears streamed down my face and church members ducked past, eyes averted in consideration for the private moment happening in public.

It's okay to be real. I could have sucked in a deep breath when she asked, put on my "church smile," answered with a vague, "It's going great, thanks!" and moved on. But that wouldn't have given me the blessing of her support, the beauty of her prayers, and the gift of gratitude I felt after purging my heart of the emotion begging for release. It wouldn't have provided permission for those kind souls who walked past us to know they could do the same one day, and it would be all right for them too.

I pray your church family can support you in this hard season, like my current church does for me now, but there's a good chance they're not prepared to. I believe churches are coming along in this area, and hopefully, you'll find somewhere that is safe to be vulnerable. I pray you find comrades in arms to help you as you process and journey along. You do need community and support, but even more than that, you *need* breath and hope from the Author of life himself. In *him*, you live and move and have your being (Acts 17:28).

Community is crucial and beneficial, but trusting and resting in the companionship we have with the Spirit is our deepest need. If you don't have your earthly community yet, you have a heavenly one, and it is sufficient. Rest in that until God moves you elsewhere.'

Something else your church family (or anyone else you meet) might not get quite right is in offering their strong, vocal opinions on your very personal future. If you haven't heard someone's opinion on divorce in general yet, you will. If you haven't heard, "Oh, your poor children," you will. And if you haven't yet been told it's a sin to remarry, even after abandonment or other biblical grounds for divorce, you will. Bless their hearts.

I heard it all—ironically, more so after I'd already gotten remarried than I did before—and it's a tough topic. Are you allowed to get remarried? Was I? There's Scripture that seems to support both sides of the argument. My logical side tells me that if my ex left me, I had no say in the decision of the divorce, and my heart still longed afterward for a godly marriage and family, I was free to remarry. I also realize our hearts will often lead us astray. Do I believe my remarriage was a sin I need to repent of? No. The way I see it is if famous theologians still debate these difficult questions, who am I to figure them all out?

There are no simple answers in these situations, but thankfully, we know the One who has the answers, and all I can do is encourage you to press into him in these matters. If I'm wrong in my view, it's the job of the Holy Spirit to reveal that to me, just as it's his job to lead you in your big decisions. So search out Scripture for yourself. Pray and ask what the Lord has for you in this season and the next one. Try not to get too stressed out about the unknown future. And don't let people in your life speak with black-and-white authority on something that is gray.

Your church might not know what to do with you right now. But Jesus does, and he's right there with you. No matter how bleak it looks, no matter how lonely it feels, no matter what specifically is happening in your marriage or heart right now . . . remember, hope *is* rising.

Sunday is coming.

Chapter 6

You Won't Walk This Perfectly

IF YOU'RE A PERFECTIONIST, THIS chapter is going to sting a little. Because here's the thing—you're not going to walk this divorce season perfectly. And you'll do more damage if you try.

The truth is, you've got to allow yourself time and space to hurt. If you're an achiever, if you thrive on productivity and accomplishment like I do (and tend to find your value in those efforts—*ouch*), this will be extra difficult.

The best part is, no one expects you to do this perfectly. That pressure you're putting on yourself to navigate this horrific nightmare in your life? That's from your own head at best, and from the devil at worst. Don't listen to it.

Have you watched the beloved TV show from the early 2000s, *Gilmore Girls*? There's an episode where the teenage girl, Rory, is going through her first relationship breakup. She's a go-getter, has Harvard on her list of life goals, reads dozens of books a month, and is incredibly mature and responsible. She decided it was silly to be heartbroken over a boy, even one she loved, so for several days after the big split, she carried on as usual. She made lists of things to accomplish and clean and organize, and she dove into multiple projects.

Her wise mother saw the folly in that and gently encouraged her several times to go ahead and fall apart, to wallow and eat the ice cream. She insisted it was part of the process, but Rory insisted with equal fervor that it was ridiculous and unnecessary . . . until one evening, after running into her ex, Rory realized it was time. With teary eyes, she came home and told her mom she was ready to wallow. So of course, her mother grabbed the ice cream and sat with her on the couch while Rory cried.[1]

Have you wallowed yet?

It looks different for everyone and doesn't have to involve ice cream. But you know the process I'm talking about—those moments where you quit trying to distract yourself and quit pushing back the tears and the shock and just cry. Grieve. Wallow.

Perhaps you've been holding back because you're afraid once you start, you won't stop. I remember that feeling. It's overwhelming. It's such a deep level of grief you wonder if it will swallow you whole, never allowing you up for air again. But you will resurface. I promise.

I've read it takes a month per every year you were married to heal. I think that's interesting . . . but also fake news. I was married a little over nine years, and I definitely wasn't fine and well after nine months. That said, I sure didn't help my timeline by making bad decisions along the way and complicating my healing process. I invited denial into my life, along with self-medicating remedies of various kinds, such as anger and retail therapy. None of it helped.

Which brings me back to my point—you aren't going to walk this perfectly (and that's okay).

When we're in seasons of heartache, we're all going to make mistakes. It's inevitable. No one handles grief perfectly—or very well, for that matter. Our judgment and discernment are clouded when we're in the middle of the storm. In dark times, we're typically behaving either with an overly active filter (overthinking everything and trying to control the uncontrollable) or with no filter at all (throwing caution to the wind and being impulsive in the effort to feel better).

You might be reading this and feeling a little discouraged, thinking, "What hope is there then? If nothing I can do will make me feel better, if wallowing is inevitable, *and* so is failure, then how am I to cope?" Here's where the hope lies.

Now the Lord is the Spirit, and where the Spirit of the Lord is, there is freedom. (2 Corinthians 3:17)

May the God of hope fill you with all joy and peace in believing, so that by the power of the Holy Spirit you may abound in hope. (Romans 15:13)

And hope does not put us to shame, because God's love has been poured into our hearts through the Holy Spirit who has been given to us. (Romans 5:5)

That's right. We have hope because of the Holy Spirit. Praise God! We aren't left to handle this level of pain and betrayal alone. The divorce that rocked your world can't shake the Firm Foundation of our lives.

That's not to say there aren't days, weeks, or even months in the process where we feel wobbly. It's like when you have an inner ear infection or are dizzy from allergies. It feels like the room is spinning when you stand up too quickly or turn your head too fast. But obviously, it's not. The room is right where it should be. Our perception is what's off.

Divorce is the same way. When you're a follower of Christ, your true foundation and security are never actually threatened. It might feel like things are spinning out of control, but it's just your temporary perspective. It will settle back down, and you'll feel sturdier than ever before.

There's something about the head-spinning that makes us appreciate the calm and cling to the Rock that much more tightly.

> **When you're a follower of Christ, your true foundation and security are never actually threatened.**

In the meantime, though, it's not uncommon to experiment with different home remedies for our dizziness. Some turn to alcohol. Others, various drugs and medications—legal or otherwise. Still others might jump into one-night stands to cure the loneliness or might try serial dating. And those are just the coping methods people talk about. There's a dozen or more smaller vices we can abuse when we're trying to medicate ourselves with something other than true hope. We can just as easily make exercise an idol, binge on TV or food to numb our thoughts, or attend every event the church has in a futile effort to make ourselves good enough. Maybe you don't seek out physical intimacy because you know you shouldn't cross that line, but your heart craves attention from the opposite sex, so you set yourself up online with a dozen different dating profiles, flirting to ease the pain.

Any of these striking a chord? You know what your coping mechanisms are. You know which ones are healthy and godly and which are prone to getting you into trouble. You won't walk this season perfectly, but there are decisions you can make that will make it much more difficult on yourself than it has to be.

Resist the temptation to self-medicate and instead wait on the Lord's healing. Quite often, prayer and time are the best remedies for a broken heart. For example, about a year ago, I was struggling with severe anxiety. I lay down one night, rolled rather abruptly onto my side, and suddenly, the room was spinning.

It continued to spin for a solid twenty-four hours.

You can imagine how much I googled in that time frame, trying to find a quick fix and a cure for the unsteadiness. I walked the hallway with hands braced against each wall. I maneuvered the stairs by sitting and scooting down them on my rear end. I couldn't shower safely. Everything was in motion, and I had no idea how to make it stop. I tried everything Google suggested (which is rarely a good idea, FYI). Nothing helped. In fact, some of my attempts to fix it myself likely only delayed the vertigo's passing.

After about a day, the dizziness finally ceased—thanks to nothing I did except waiting it out and trying to relax.

In the same way, when your circumstances and reality are spinning around you, there is no quick fix. Turning to vices and impulsive decisions feels like a quick fix, but it's only an illusion that delays true healing. These things mask the root issue and only address the surface-level emotions. For example: If we want to be stronger, we go to the gym and lift weights, right? But weight lifting results in sore muscles. If we stopped going to the gym, the pain would cease. Yet our goal would be that much further out of reach. We have to get past the initial waves of discomfort to reach our ultimate, long-game goals.

Which brings me back to the topic of the Holy Spirit. He is our *only* steady anchor in the chaos. And if that fact is new for you, follow me down this road for a moment.

The denomination I grew up in was typically heavy on Scripture and light on the Holy Spirit. The first is great, the latter, not so much. Of course, no church will get it right all the time, but in this darkest season of life, we need the whole package. We need Scripture poured into us, *and* we need the presence of the Holy Spirit to minister to our broken hearts.

God is good, and he gave me that whole package.

He led me to a ministry group that became such a healing place. One night, the pastor, Bobby, was preaching on the Holy Spirit. So much of what was being said was new to me but was right there in the pages of Scripture. My interest was piqued, my heart hammering. I knew God had something for me that evening, but at that point in my journey, I was afraid to even hope. I'd been through so much and had been so disappointed, it seemed safer to stay numb. But then Bobby asked if anyone in our group wanted to pray for a fresh outpouring of the Holy Spirit, and everything in me shouted *yes*.

Still, I hesitated. In my denomination, we believed that when you are drawn to the Lord in salvation, you're filled with the Holy Spirit right then, and it's a one-and-done type of thing. He's always with you from that day forward.

I still believe that, but I also know what happened that night.

When a young man and I both answered in the affirmative, the group split. The men gathered around the guy, and the women gathered around me a few pews over. Sitting there on that padded bench seat, surrounded by fellow sisters in Christ of various denominations and ages ranging from late teens to early thirties, I braced my elbows on my knees and buried my face in my hands as they began to pray over me.

Their hands on my back felt warm through my thin hoodie as they prayed, some whispering prayers in the Spirit and some praying out loud in English. They all asked the Lord to flood me with his Spirit. Immediately, waves of heat coursed over my body, and my back felt like it was on fire in the best way possible. Flames of heat engulfed me, sending trickles of sweat down my spine. My face warmed, and everything inside me welled up with agreement. *Yes, Lord.*

I don't have all the answers about what happened that night. If you're in the charismatic circles, you're probably nodding with a knowing smile. If you're not, you might be optimistically skeptical, as I would be had it not happened directly to me.

Theologically, I don't know how to explain it, except there was a definite shift in my heart that day that has been maintained to the moment I'm writing this paragraph. Somehow, through the Lord's sovereignty, the Holy Spirit clearly communicated his constant presence. Some might say I was baptized with the Holy Spirit. Others would choose different wording, and still others will probably skip past this page altogether. But you know what? Without that fresh reminder of who the Holy Spirit is and how he works in my life, I don't know how I would have survived the following months.

God knew what I needed and exactly when I needed it, and he chose that moment and that method. And, my friend, he knows exactly what you need and when you need it. God is never early, but he is also never late with his goodness. We must trust him and his process.

Looking back, I can clearly see how God's fingerprints were all over the calendar of those years of divorce and post-divorce healing. Now, I can easily detect the pattern he created, the order of circumstances that at the time felt unnecessary, painful, or random. He was incredibly intentional with me, orchestrating the people I encountered, the sermons I heard, and the books I read, all because he loves me. In that season of my life, *nothing* was more important than knowing I was still loved. Abandoned by one, but never alone. Rejected by one, but so very chosen.

> **God knows exactly what you need and when you need it.**

And he is working the same in your life. He's not threatened by denominational differences or preferences. He is good, he is God, and he is sovereign. He's fully in control of your story. He has a plan for you and your future, and I know that because you're still here—you still have breath. Those breaths might be ragged and full of pain, but they're coming—rising and falling in your chest, and for believers, the Holy Spirit is right there with each inhale and exhale (1 Corinthians

3:16). He is real and alive and working on your behalf. He is interceding for you (Romans 8:26–27), helping you (John 14:26), and giving you joy (1 Thessalonians 1:6).

Don't give up hoping for the other side. Don't give in to discouragement or the lie that God has given up on you. And on the days when your grasp of this truth feels slack, remember—he's got you.

You won't walk this path perfectly. But you can walk it with him.

Chapter 7

Faith Under Fire

My mobile home in the country had a nice bathroom. That's the best part about manufactured homes—so much space! (Until you're the one solely in charge of maintaining all that space and mowing three acres with a five-year-old on your lap. But I digress.) Long showers quickly became one of my post-divorce habits. I could get my kiddo set up with a cartoon or her educational handheld game and take as much time as I needed to pray privately and cry alone. I remember often quieting my heart and asking God to tell me if he was going to put my marriage back together. I'd position my face right against the seam of the shower door, where the steam from the hot water collided with the air conditioning streaming in from the bathroom, and I'd ask. Seek. Cry.

Wait.

At the time, I believed deep down that God told me we would be reconciled. I know now it was more likely my own heart simply believing what it needed to in order to survive. That's the tricky part. Listening to the Lord without letting our own desires overshadow truth. I knew that Scripture was my most reliable source for hearing from God. But obviously there wasn't a chapter and verse referencing whether my husband was going to return to our marriage. For a long time, I needed the answer to be yes.

But eventually, I came to the point where I wanted to *know* something for sure, whatever the answer. Living in limbo, wondering how to proceed with our lives, is perhaps the hardest part of the entire process. There are so many unanswered questions. *Will my ex ever file for divorce officially? Will he ever come back? Should I file first to protect myself financially? What about our money and community property? What if he keeps refusing to pay half the mortgage? Where will my daughter and I go? When will we reach a custody arrangement?* And that was only the half of it.

No matter how hard I prayed or how long I waited in that shower, I never seemed to hear from God. I didn't feel alone, necessarily. I knew he was with me, though some days I felt that truth more than others. But I still didn't have answers.

You might be stuck in that very long season of waiting right now too. Where you don't know whether it's wise or naive to keep hoping. Where you don't know what to do, how to prepare, or what to think. There's this part of your heart that wants to brace for the worst while hoping for the best, but you think somehow you'll manifest the divorce into officially happening if you stop hoping.

You're putting all this pressure on yourself in the waiting season. That's completely unnecessary but, at the same time, almost impossible to stop. I wish I could hug you in this stage. It's a very hard one, and I'm sorry.

When you're an imaginative person like myself, it's especially easy to fill in all those blanks in the waiting period with your own what-ifs and potential solutions. All of which typically make it worse, by the way. I didn't know what was going to happen, still wasn't entirely sure what *had* happened, and I had no idea what to do next . . . or if I should do anything at all.

I was a confused hot mess, running on coffee, very little sleep, and sheer determination to keep going as a single mom. To make matters worse, in this stage, emotions swing like a pendulum from "forget my husband, I don't even care anymore" protective-type measures to real, gut-wrenching, soul-deep anguish and sobs. Because of my quest for answers and my spiritual crossroads of trying to understand who was really in charge of this divorce mess—God or my ex—I reached a point where something had to give.

Does that resonate? Do you need a boost? Rest? Answers? I know I did. I needed a reset on my heart.

So I did what any normal person would do—I asked a new girl at work if she wanted to go with me to pray with monks.

Let me explain.

I'd just finished reading *Found* by Micha Boyett. Ann Voskamp wrote the foreword and talked about her experience praying in a Benedictine monastery—how it had cork tiles and so did her own kitchen and how all of life is holy ground for the believer.[1] Something in my soul hitched a little. I didn't know how or why, but I knew I needed to go pray.

In a monastery.

If you've ever walked through a divorce, you know this makes as much sense as anything else you think during that time period. If you haven't, then I pray you never understand. But it was an answer. Granted, it was a weird answer and certainly not one I expected when I prayed about what was next, but it was a direction that felt hand-delivered from God.

I googled and found a nearby working monastery in Arkansas called Subiaco Abbey. It was within driving distance for me, and—score—visitors were welcome during certain times of the day. So I took a deep breath, then went and asked my new friend Cat if she'd want to go with me.

Miracle of miracles, Cat said yes. I truly wouldn't have blamed her if she'd instead blocked my phone number and quit her job to get away from her weirdo coworker!

Since my husband had left me, I'd done quite a few impulsive things. I bought a violin that I had zero idea how to play (still don't). I got my first tattoo and a bright yellow Camaro. I even volunteered with a ministry that witnessed to women working in strip clubs. This decision to visit a monastery might have been the most random one on my list yet, but somehow in my spirit, it felt exactly on time.

Cat and I made plans to go a few weekends later. Then, upon closer inspection, I realized the abbey we intended to visit was the *exact same one* Ann Voskamp had visited and referred to in the foreword of *Found*. My second miracle.

So we booked our B and B, which according to the website was owned by an older couple, doubled as a winery, and was the only lodging available within a reasonable distance of the abbey. We were off!

The weekend started out as a comedy of errors—we got a late start, got lost, and finally arrived at the B and B late into the night, where we were greeted by a kind but most eccentric B and B owner who insisted on giving us a tour of the place despite the late hour. When we stepped inside the tiny chapel on the vineyard grounds (where he told us Mother Teresa once sat), we ducked our heads in respect. Then he casually proceeded to tell us that his wife's remains were buried beneath that exact chapel.

Our adventure was starting strong. I won't even go into how our shared room lacked a bathroom door but had a secret passage that led to who knows where.

We survived the night despite the odds (maybe the third miracle?) and set out early for the abbey. The moment I stepped onto the grounds, my spirit quickened. Have you ever been somewhere and felt in your core that you were supposed to be in that very place at that very moment in time? I recognize, and wholly attest to, the sovereignty of God.

All my days are numbered and ordained. But that particular morning, I *felt* that truth deep in my gut rather than simply believing it.

You might have to put yourself in an unexpected place to grab hold of that secure, I-*know*-God-exists feeling. Reaching that moment of connection and gut truth with the Lord often requires getting outside your comfort zone so your senses are heightened. Your heart is open. And the distractions of the everyday are muted. Get where the veil is thinner for you.

> **You might have to put yourself in an unexpected place to grab hold of that secure, I-*know*-God-exists feeling.**

October leaves whispered under our feet as Cat and I checked in and received a schedule of prayer. We had a bit of time before the next prayer session, so we wandered the grounds, breathing in cool air and breathing out stress. We met cows and stood outside a graveyard, drank in the beauty of multiple stained-glass windows, walked through the cloisters, and silently snapped pictures I still treasure to this day.

Then it was time to pray.

Cat and I sat in the back of the chapel, listening to the rhythmic, lulling sounds of the monks chanting and singing their daily routine. Familiar, yet no less reverent. This was their entire life, and since my own felt foreign to me at that time, I soaked it in.

Sometimes, God lets you hide and grieve silently in the shadows. Other times, he launches you out of your comfort zone by having a monk call you to the front of the church and place you in the cathedral stall with the other monks.

Guess which time this was?

Cat and I shot each other "uh-oh" looks as we slowly made our way down the aisle as instructed, taking our seats on the wooden pew on the platform with the robe-clad men. We mouthed the words we didn't know as the swell of praise and worship rose around us, and my heart went from feeling awkward to feeling like I belonged. While my theology most likely differed from that of the men around me, my song to God was the same. And we were united in that melody. I felt connected to the Lord in a fresh way.

Several songs and prayers later, we took Communion, then filed out of the chapel, my heart airy and light. Oh, there was nothing magical about the abbey or the men living and worshipping there. Nothing extra special about the shared Communion cup or the routine or the grounds. The cork tiles beneath my feet, which I also took a picture of, were not any more holy ground than my own kitchen floor. Both had seen my tears and had soaked them up.

But *that* was what my heart had so desperately needed—to recognize that God was still there, even when my prayers felt unheard. Even when they were unspoken. And God is there for you, too, even in your silence. Even when you're trying to hide in the back of the church or you're avoiding church altogether. When our faith is doused with doubt and our hearts wrung out, God is still there. He was, he is, everywhere. That recognition thrust upon me a whole new appreciation for Psalm 139:7. "Where shall I go from your Spirit? Or where shall I flee from your presence?" We may not intend to hide, but sometimes our souls need the reminder that we literally can't anyway.

God isn't going to leave you. Never has. Never will.

Even though I'd initially tried to hide in the back pew of that cathedral, God showed me that he orchestrated my steps. And with those first footfalls down the church aisle toward the chanting monks came my first step forward into fully acknowledging God was still in control, even among my husband's choices and my grief.

Jesus had me, and I wasn't getting away.

⋮ God isn't going to leave you. Never has.
⋮ Never will.

Have you been trying to hide? Are you sitting in plain sight in the back of the figurative church, unable to come closer because of fear or uncertainty? Do you doubt God wants you nearby? I think of Adam and Eve when they hid in the garden of Eden. They were guilty, yet God pursued them and called them to come forth. I think of Jesus ushering an unsure Zacchaeus (who was shunned by his people too) from the tree or extending a hand to Peter on the waves when the disciple's fear got the best of him.

God calls for *you*.

That's present tense, right now—God calls for you.

Consider this as you debate making your way down the proverbial aisle. The monks in that abbey continually seek to live as pure a life as they possibly can, and even then, they're still sinners. They're still born depraved like every other human since Adam and Eve. Yet daily, they sing and offer praise and prayer to the Lord. Their failures and shortcomings don't hinder their main goal and priority in life—to worship.

Your hurt and grief and uncertainty shouldn't hinder that either. Don't wait until you have your life, circumstances, and heart all tidied up before you come to God. One might even argue it's precisely when we're unsure and messy that we need to draw the nearest.

Leaving the abbey that afternoon, my heart breathed a sigh of relief at obtaining an answer to a question I hadn't realized I needed to ask. My experience there revealed that final, blessed, core-deep truth—not only would Jesus never leave me, but I also didn't want to get away. Sure, I'd wanted to run from the new circumstances I'd been thrust into, but never from Jesus. As crushed and broken as I'd felt those last several months, I didn't want to hide from the One who knew me inside out.

Is your faith under fire? Is your foundation threatened by the persistent onslaught of questions and doubt? Mine was. But at Subiaco Abbey, I found a *true* hiding place.

In Christ alone.

There's room there for you too, friend. Stop striving to get answers to the questions you think you're asking, and silence your heart for the true source of clarity. Maybe that's discovered in a prayer box with monks while clutching a Communion cup, or in your living room while clutching your favorite coffee mug.

He's not going anywhere. And if you're in him, you aren't either. He's holding you even when your grip is too shaky to return his hold.

Chapter 8

Unlikely Romance in Unlikely Places

You MIGHT HAVE SKIPPED TO this chapter thinking I was going to give a juicy tell-all of my new marriage. This is not that chapter. (Don't stop reading though!) This chapter is way more important than that one.

I need to tell you a secret.

Remember when I shared with you about the night my ex left? How the trailer floor pressed unforgivingly against my knees and I couldn't breathe but I could pray the name of Jesus? I always tear up when I tell that story. Those tears used to flow because the pain of my husband leaving rubbed fresh with the memory. Now, I tear up solely because of the joy of recognizing how intentionally seen and held I was by my heavenly Father.

And that's what we want, isn't it? We want to be seen, held, protected. Oh sure, we all have our warrior moments. We can be fierce and strong and independent. We have to be sometimes. But it's there, deep down, wired in us since Eden . . . we were meant to be loved and cherished. We were meant to be romanced. This manifests in different ways for each of us, but that desire is there.

Think about it. What is romance to you? It could be your significant other planning a night out and arranging childcare or sending you flowers. Your date offering to mow the yard or your spouse doing the dishes. A surprise note tucked into your purse or overnight bag. It looks different for everyone, but as humans, we're designed to want a form of it.

⠿ We were meant to be loved and cherished.

When we go through a severe breakup or an unwanted divorce, we will often default to self-preservation mode and attempt to starve our built-in romance desire. I remember the moment I realized my husband leaving wasn't a phase—he was really gone and most likely was not coming back. And it hit me that I wasn't going to be kissed for a long time. It seems like such an odd thing to think about in the midst of much bigger issues, but I remember breaking down and texting my cousin, sobbing over the grief of losing the gift of a simple kiss. I was a romance author, on deadline for a romance novel, and was starved for romance.

But our desire for earthly, human romance can't ever be fully fulfilled on this earth . . . and it's unlikely to die off, because it's been engraved in each of us since creation. It's our reflection of the very image of God. Genesis 1:27 (NIV) says, "So God created mankind in his own image, in the image of God he created them; male and female he created them."

All women want romance, but for those of us who have walked through divorce, it's a different kind of longing. We aren't just longing for what we want, we're longing for what we *lost*, for what we once knew and are deeply fearful we will never know again.

Then, to make it harder, on top of those longings lies the sting of rejection. As divorced women, we are filled with the lingering insecurity of whether or not we're worthy of romance anymore. It's a heartbreaking place—not to mention a dangerous place. That's when the hiding starts. We try to protect our battered hearts beneath layers of bitterness, baggy clothes, disdain, unforgiveness, eating disorders, or a cram-packed schedule. If the heart can't be seen or caught, it can't be rejected, right? We women know how to hide.

Ask Eve.

But guess what? God sees. And he longs to catch your heart every time. Just like he came for Eve in the garden after the first sin rocked the world—just like he came for me on the floor of my double-wide—he comes for you. He comes to woo, to draw you near, to comfort. To encourage. To cradle your heart in nail-scarred hands.

As a woman made in God's image, have you ever considered that God desires romance too? He invented it. He *is* love.

Read these verses and let them wash over you. Bask in their meaning. Don't skip over this, friend. You need it. In fact, I challenge you to read them out loud.

> But then I will win her back once again.
>> I will lead her into the desert
>> and speak tenderly to her there.
> I will return her vineyards to her
>> and transform the Valley of Trouble into a gateway of hope.
> She will give herself to me there,
>> as she did long ago when she was young,
>> when I freed her from her captivity in Egypt.
>> (Hosea 2:14–15 NLT)

As the Father has loved me, so have I loved you. Abide in my love. (John 15:9)

But God shows his love for us in that while we were still sinners, Christ died for us. (Romans 5:8)

Who shall separate us from the love of Christ? Shall tribulation, or distress, or persecution, or famine, or nakedness, or danger, or sword? (Romans 8:35)

For I am sure that neither death nor life, nor angels nor rulers, nor things present nor things to come, nor powers, nor height nor depth, nor anything else in all creation, will be able to separate us from the love of God in Christ Jesus our Lord. (Romans 8:38–39)

But God, being rich in mercy, because of the great love with which he loved us, even when we were dead in our trespasses, made us alive together with Christ—by grace you have been saved—and raised us up with him and seated us with him in the heavenly places in Christ Jesus. (Ephesians 2:4–6)

God loves us. God loves *you*. And he put that longing for romance in us to reveal his heart for us. Why else would chivalrous gestures resonate so deeply? Why else, when we read books or watch movies where someone sacrifices for the person they love, do our chests swell and our throats knot? We're wired to do so—because Jesus sacrificed it all for us.

The Bible calls us, as believers, the bride of Christ. Can you imagine the freedom we'd experience if we let down our guard and asked God to romance us? I'm not talking about the cringey, early 2000s Christianese "Jesus is my boyfriend" kind of thing. I'm talking the mature, biblical "the Lord your Maker is your husband" kind of thing.

Isaiah 54:5 says, "For your Maker is your husband, the LORD of hosts is his name; and the Holy One of Israel is your Redeemer, the God of the whole earth he is called."

If that happened—if we truly trusted God to meet the romance-longing parts of our hearts—the equation would be complete. We would have romance *and* God would have our hearts—unhindered, undistracted, fully engaged. In that scenario, we would have the whole package of fulfillment and contentment.

Unfortunately, we live in denial of this truth, thanks to a combination of culture, society, and the devil's attempts to convince us it's not enough. Satan's goal is to convince us that God's version of romance isn't sufficient. That God himself isn't enough. That we need something or someone else—namely, a man.

Before you think I'm slamming the idea of earthly marriage, hear me out. Marriage is a gift. God ordained it in the garden. But its ultimate purpose is to reflect the bigger, grander marriage of Christ and his bride. Inside our bond with the church and God is where we find true union. We can be spiritually fulfilled and still single on earth. We can also be spiritually *un*fulfilled and married on earth. Marriage is not a requirement for contentment—relationship with Christ is.

Remember that romance novel deadline I mentioned? I wrote the second book in that contract while still healing and raw from divorce. It's titled *Love Arrives in Pieces*, and I call it the book of my heart because it features my first divorced heroine. In the story, Stella tries to hide too. A divorced preacher's kid and former pageant queen, Stella decides her beauty was a curse, and yet without it, she's nothing. After all, her husband saw the real her beneath the layers of makeup, bronzer, and sequins, and he bailed. Her beauty wasn't enough, but she has no idea who she is without it—and is even more afraid to find out. What if she still isn't enough as she is? So she dabbles in art, a secret passion, because deep down, she longs to make something beautiful that won't fade.

But God has other plans for Stella. He hasn't forgotten her, and as Stella releases the broken pieces of her heart to him, God prepares a beautiful masterpiece of mosaic tiles—beauty from the broken.

I believe God has that same plan for all of us, regardless of whether marital restoration or remarriage is in our future as divorcées. Our job is to simply let go of the pieces. When we keep a death grip on the individual shards, we're only going to cut our hands.

Surrender those broken fragments of your past, your fears, your memories, your heart, and let him do what only he can do—create beauty from ashes. This means giving up your idea of what your future looks like and trusting God to work out his plan instead. Surrendering is messy—there's usually tears. Pain. Even anger. But letting go of a dream makes way for a new one, and while God isn't a genie, he's very much in the business of dream granting.

So long as we trust him to bring his plans to pass.

And in the meantime, while you're surrendering and adjusting what your dream looks like, God can romance your heart in ways that put mortal men to shame. Who created romance in the first place? Who created breathtaking sunsets and crimson roses and wild horses and intricate snowflakes?

> **While God isn't a genie, he's very much in the business of dream granting.**

Instead of grieving the loss of earthly romantic things like I did early on in my process, I challenge you to ask the Lord to meet those needs in your heart. Right now. Shut this book and pray. Ask God to romance you in a unique and special way just between the two of you. Ask specifically for him to provide you with what I call an inside joke—something between just you and him that has special meaning. Something he can send you when you're low and hurting, something that will bolster your faith in those weak moments when the fear and pain take over. For some, it's butterflies. For others, it's a particular flower or a song, hummingbirds or the color purple.

He always sent me hearts.

Hearts in concrete stains and in clouds and rocks and random pieces of paper appearing in my bed or on my floor. Hearts in the vegetables in my soup and in rain puddles on the ground. He never, not once, failed to provide one when I came to him pleading. One time in my divorce season I was pumping gas at a station and was near an emotional crash. I had that tight throat, tears-pressing-my-eyes kind of thing going on, and was about to lose it right there on pump three. I was weary, sad, and done. Then I looked down to see a giant oil stain on the concrete in a perfect heart shape. So instead of sobbing, I started laughing, then crying at the same time. I was a complete hot mess, but I had joy and hope.

Jesus came for me.

We long for that hero to save us. But what we're really longing for isn't a knight in shining armor, but rather one who is battle-scarred and has proven his merit. We desire someone by our side to fight for us, to be willing to go the distance to protect us, provide for us, and even die for us. That's part of what hurts so badly when husbands leave. Divorce means they stopped fighting.

But guess what? Jesus has two battle-scarred hands and a sword-pierced side. He's already proven his love for you by literally dying for you. It doesn't get more romantic than that. Unlike the love of your ex or mine, God's love isn't conditional. His affection doesn't run out. His love is not based on performance or physical beauty or ideals. It's not just enough, it's *more than* enough.

My advice? Put down the Rocky Road (okay, one more bite) and pick up your Bible. Set down your phone and kneel in prayer. Ask Jesus to meet you in your need for romance. He will eagerly pursue your heart—and you'll know love and fulfillment in ways you never dreamed possible.

Because even if you get remarried to a wonderful, godly man like I eventually did, you will still have unmet desires in your heart. No man can fulfill you completely. A good husband is a gift and a blessing—and if you have a desire for that, absolutely pray for it and trust the Lord for his timing. But don't believe the lie that getting remarried is the only path to the fulfillment of your heart.

The best news is that you can have your needs met today, right now, by going to the Lord—regardless of your earthly relationship status.

Chapter 9

Step Away from the Pen

WHOEVER SAYS GOD DOESN'T HAVE a sense of humor has clearly never gone through anything difficult. I don't mean that irreverently. I mean it literally. Some of the funniest things happened during my darkest season of divorce. And not just laugh-out-loud moments, but irony or things others might chalk up to coincidence that I know are otherwise.

There are several instances where the humor wasn't evident until years after the fact. Such as the time my husband had only been moved out for a few months, and I happened to look down while washing my hair in the shower and saw something that most definitely was not supposed to be sitting on the drain between my feet.

A scorpion.

Let's just say the arachnid didn't make it, and he probably also went deaf before he kicked the proverbial bucket (RIP). That poor creature represented everything unfair in that season of my life and really got it.

Or the time when another wildlife creature burrowed up under the lining of my trailer and died, and Billy the Exterminator's (remember that show?) nephew had to come dig it out. (Yes, that experience was as gross as it sounds.)

Possibly the most ironic was the time when I almost canceled a first date with a nice single dad because I was so fed up with the entire dating process (more on that to come) but then ended up going anyway and eventually marrying him.

It's amusing how God works. Folks often refer to Christianity as the upside-down kingdom. Things typically don't go the way we expect or hope. Jesus talked about how the least will be made great and the great will be made small. In the upside-down kingdom, leaders serve. Humility is advancement. Sacrifice is honored. Less is more. And in losing our life, we gain it. The rules of the world don't work in the church. We can't walk with Christ and be in union with other believers if we're power hungry, greedy, money obsessed, and striving to be on top.

I found these upside-down rules are also true in my love life. The world will try to convince you to strive, to put yourself out there, to ask men out and flaunt what you have. But the more I tried to force things on my own, the worse off I became. The harder I tried to convince my ex to come back and the more I tried to force things into being, the farther away it all felt.

Giving in to the temptation to lie, get revenge, or manipulate only makes us feel worse and further from God. For me, my ex seemed to be thriving with no consequences of his abandonment, and it all felt so horribly unfair. I wavered between wanting him to get what he deserved and feeling outright broken over his choices.

But you can't fight sin with sin.

The sooner I let go—the sooner I surrendered the future I'd imagined and the plans I'd made to a blank page instead—the sooner God began to write something beautiful. It was God's story after all, and I'm not a main character. Neither are you. All the hardships in this life are to give glory to God and make us more like Christ. Apparently, in God's plan, there was more glory to be had from me walking this horrible season out. I had to trust the long-term picture I couldn't fully see.

He has a plan for you too, and as hard as it might be, it's filled with moments of humor, irony, and snorts. It's a story worth reading and living, and your part isn't over yet. Some chapters feel like they will never end (I write romance novels—ask me how I know!) and yet, eventually, they do. Something wonderful might be on the next page.

In fiction writing, we're taught to leave readers on a hook at the end of every scene or chapter. We're not supposed to wrap things up neatly, because the reader will be able to stop reading and might not pick the book back up for a while. The goal is to keep them turning pages.

Sometimes I wonder if God pens our lives that way. How boring of a book—or a life—it would be if everything went according to plan! How dull for there to never be any conflict, character arc, or growth. The Lord is the Author and Finisher of our faith, and he intricately weaves details of romance, drama, humor, suspense, and inspiration into our stories. (Our lives tend to be every genre at once, don't they?)

Just like I, as a fiction author, bring my characters through trials and tribulations to shape them into better people by the end of the book, God uses affliction in our lives to mold us to be more like him (Psalm 119:67, 71; James 1:2–4).

And as often as we tend to forget it, that's the *real* goal of our lives.

Think back with me. As little girls, many of us dreamed of our wedding day, didn't we? We planned our flowers and picked accent colors and imagined what song would play as we strolled down the aisle. When we got older, those details changed a dozen times, and as friendships came and went over our adolescent years, we mentally edited our list of bridesmaids. Yet our wedding was always on our radar—and eventually, as we got older, so was the thought of the actual marriage. Where we would live, where we would honeymoon, what careers we might have, whether we'd have kids and, if so, how many. We dreamed of growing old together and sitting on the porch sipping coffee and laughing about the antics of our grandkids.

Because we women spend so much of our pre-married lives focusing on all things wedding- and marriage-related, it can be more than a little jolting to suddenly see it all end. It's easy to feel as though we've lost our entire identity. All those dreams and handwritten lists and journals filled with planning? Suddenly irrelevant. It can feel like it was all for nothing.

And we tend to wonder who we are if we're no longer a wife.

Yet when we step back and recognize our lives are for a bigger purpose than solely marriage and that our identities are not only found in being wives, we can finally have hope for the next chapter—whatever it looks like.

Just do yourself a favor and remember who is writing the story: the One who not only created you but loves you and is pursuing you with good things in mind.

During a particularly hard week in my divorce season, I literally wrote, "Drop the pen," on a sticky note and taped it on my computer as a reminder to myself to stop trying to take over and write my own story. God's version was so much richer and more layered and intentional. Sort of like the difference between a rough draft and a published copy—which would you rather read? Trust me. You do not want the rough draft.

> **Remember who is writing the story: the One who not only created you but loves you and is pursuing you with good things in mind.**

Is there an area of your life where you need to drop the pen? Where you are striving to force things to happen in your way and your timing? It's probably not going so well, is it? Maybe you're dating prematurely and trying to convince yourself someone is right for you when they're clearly not. Or you've written off men forever and are harboring bitterness in your heart, but the desire to be a wife just won't die no matter how hard you try to kill it.

Wherever your heart is, be honest—with yourself, with God, and with others. Remember, it's possible to deeply desire a dream to come true and genuinely surrender your will to God's at the same time.

Here's what happened when I finally did.

During my search to find the right church, I ended up attending Sunday school at one and services at another—in two different denominations. I was still trying to discover where I fit and where I could serve and grow in my new identity as a single mom. Then the church where I attended Sunday school officially brought on a full-time pastor (they'd been in an interim season for years), and I felt very drawn to Pastor John and his wife, Gretchan. I loved how Pastor John preached expositorily through the Bible and how full of life Gretchan was and how unashamedly she worshipped.

One Sunday morning, I met with them after church to introduce myself and share a little of my story. With a cracked voice and teary eyes, I briefly ran through my divorce situation and told how I was a single mom and had made some mistakes on my recent dating journey. How badly I longed for marriage and a full family for my daughter. How I was trusting God for my dreams but battling fear at the same time. How wearying it could be.

They were immediately sympathetic and encouraging and welcomed me into the congregation with open arms. They even asked if they could pray for me right then. Of course I agreed, and as they hovered over me, Gretchan prayed. She thanked the Lord for bringing me to the church and then pleaded with God to send me a godly husband and to answer the prayers of my heart. While she spoke, Pastor John whispered over us, "Let it be, Lord. Let it be."

There are moments in life that seem to engrave themselves upon our hearts, and that was one of them for me. Even now, I can bring back that prayerful moment in vivid detail. The feel of the pew under my dress, the fierce grip of Gretchan's hands on mine, the tears burning the back of my throat. Something was happening in that moment—I knew it as surely as I knew my name and my address and that scorpions didn't belong in showers. I couldn't prove it, but I *knew*.

Fast-forward a few short months, and my brand-new boyfriend was attending that same church with me and playing drums in worship. Then that boyfriend proposed, and when I walked the aisle at my wedding, I had a charm dangling off my bouquet with the words "Let It Be" stamped in the metal. Pastor John officiated, Gretchan rejoiced . . . and I wondered how big the Lord's smile was.

I know not every story ends that way. There's no guarantee that your marriage will be restored or that you'll marry a new spouse. There are no promises that things will go the way you want or when you want them to. Divorce is one very unfortunate element of a broken, fallen world.

But God always has the final say.

And he is good.

I love Ephesians 3:20–21: "Now to him who is able to do far more abundantly than all that we ask or think, according to the power at work within us, to him be glory in the church and in Christ Jesus throughout all generations, forever and ever. Amen."

> **God always has the final say. And he is good.**

God has plans you can't imagine right now. He isn't done with you yet, my friend. The story isn't over. There are chapters to be written, and I can guarantee that as you walk this journey with him, there will be blessings. There will be moments of laugh-out-loud humor if you'll look for them. There will be tears of grief but also tears of joy. There will be moments of irony and exclamations of praise and shouts of unbelief.

I never could have predicted what would come next as I sat on that pew praying with my pastor and his wife. They couldn't have either.

But God knew from the beginning the exact timeline and was working in my heart along the way.

He's working in yours. So deep breaths. It's safe to surrender. He's a really, really good writer.

And remember, even if your marriage isn't restored, *you* can be. You *will* be. Just press into him and keep turning the pages he's so carefully and intentionally written for you. Psalm 139:16 says, "Your eyes saw my unformed substance; in your book were written, every one of them, the days that were formed for me, when as yet there was none of them." God is writing your story, and in its own unique, personalized way . . . it's going to be a best seller.

You're not finished—and that's no joke.

Chapter 10

If You Can't Say Something Nice . . . Try Painting

WORDS ARE FUNNY THINGS, AREN'T they?

They seem so harmless at first, but they affect us deeply—especially when wielded with the wrong tone or expressed at the wrong time.

The Bible has a lot to say about the power of words too.

Proverbs 25:11 says, "A word fitly spoken is like apples of gold in a setting of silver." What a beautiful image. Apples and gold and silver. Saying the right thing at the right time is such a blessing and a gift, especially for those going through hardship.

Also consider Proverbs 18:21: "Death and life are in the power of the tongue, and those who love it will eat its fruits." That got serious quickly. Our tongues have power to bring death or give life. Not literal death or life, of course—we're not the Lord. But figuratively, what we say can affect another person on a soul-deep level and either boost their spirits or keep them downcast in the pit.

This passage in Matthew is another grave eye-opener. "For out of the abundance of the heart the mouth speaks. The good person out of his good treasure brings forth good, and the evil person out of his evil treasure brings forth evil. I tell you, on the day of judgment people will give account for every careless word they speak, for by your words you will be justified, and by your words you will be condemned" (12:34–37).

Yikes. Our words are not meant to be flippantly thrown around and then forgotten. There's not an easily dismissed "Well, we were in a fight, that doesn't count" type of excuse for what we say. We're responsible for the words we speak—and on top of that, the Bible makes it clear our words come from deep inside. Like a toothpaste tube provides toothpaste when squeezed, what resides in our hearts oozes out when we speak. And neither ugly words nor toothpaste can be put back in!

It's easy to point the finger at others and accuse them of not speaking well to us during seasons of hardship or grief. After all, I'm sure we've all encountered That Person at some time or another. You know, the one who says horrible things at the wrong time, thinking it's funny. The one who jokes about things too soon, or who is truly oblivious and always manages to make an awkward situation worse.

For example, when I was expecting my daughter, there was an usher at my old church who thought it was hilarious to ask me every Sunday for the final three months of my pregnancy if I was sure it wasn't twins (facepalm).

If you're going through a divorce, you've most likely encountered people like this. They might mean well, but words can cut. And the wound seems to go a little deeper when you're already bleeding. You might smile or fake laugh in the moment, but inside, you're cringing and wishing for escape.

Oh, how I remember. You've had people ask how you're doing but not stick around for the answer. And you've had people be nosy and ask what happened to end your marriage, as if they're sitting down for a drama on PBS with popcorn rather than inquiring about your very real life. You've walked up on whispered conversations that hushed when you arrived. And you've been given offers to talk by people who don't bother to answer the phone when you call.

Though honestly, even if I had a script to give someone, I don't know what it would say. Because in those rough moments, everything is a dichotomy. You want encouragement, but you don't want false hope. You want someone to assure you, but you realize they can't guarantee things they don't know. You want someone to be angry on your behalf, but if they say something against your ex, you still feel defensive and have a confusing urge to protect him.

There are no easy answers. At the end of the day, a broken heart just takes time to heal, and sometimes having someone sit with you in silence is the greatest gift of all.

Just like we want others to be gentle and careful with us, we need to start by being gentle and careful with ourselves. I can't help but ask—what words are you speaking to yourself in this season? What are you saying to the mirror? Are you being compassionate with the woman you see peering back at you, or are you being harsh and dismissive with her? Maybe you're not speaking out loud to yourself, so you aren't even sure what you're saying. But if you take a minute and sit in silence, you'll hear the soundtrack running through your mind of how you think of yourself—and those are still words. Other people can't hear them, but your heart does. They count.

Proverbs 11:17 applies to what you say about others and what you say about yourself: "A man who is kind benefits himself, but a cruel man hurts himself."

Here's a challenge. Take a day and write down every negative thought about yourself that tries to invade your mind. Anything negative you hear about your heart, your worth, your value, your body, or your self-image . . . write it down, in all its ugly glory.

Then go back in the evening and counter those negative thoughts with the truth of Scripture. If you hear that you're not valuable, write down a verse that talks about being made in the image of God (Genesis 9:6). If you are fighting the lie that you're not desirable, seek out a verse that tells you the truth about your beauty and write it down (1 Peter 3:3–4).

> **"A man who is kind benefits himself, but a cruel man hurts himself."**

When you're done, compile your list somewhere handy, where you can see it and read it over and over. You're going to drown out the lies with truth.

You're going to be nice to yourself.

And being nice to yourself might also mean becoming vocal about what you need. Remember, right now, people aren't always going to know what to say to you. It's okay that you need different things at different times, and it's okay to tell your friends and family that some truths hurt too much right now to think about.

Don't give up on your friends, even if they don't get it right in this hard season. Remember, any gesture of genuine care is better than no gesture at all. They're trying. If you can help them help you, then do it. Be specific. Speak up for what you need—and what you don't need. Be honest and real. Everyone will be the better for it.

I remember desperately wanting to vent and have support but also not wanting to say too many negative things about my ex because I was so hopeful we would get back together. I wanted to protect him. What if our marriage was restored but everyone stayed mad at him for what happened? What if I said too much I couldn't take back? What if my friends or family held grudges and didn't forgive even after I did? I ended up keeping a lot to myself initially and thought I might explode from the pain.

Looking back, there was also an element of denial going on within that decision—if I didn't talk about the divorce too much, I wouldn't have to admit it was happening. But I was shell-shocked. My world had tilted, and I needed support. My thoughts were racing wild, and I would work myself into a panic trying to figure everything out alone in my head. Slowly, I started opening up to a few close friends I trusted, giving myself more opportunities to process the drastic life changes I was experiencing. This provided them the chance to breathe life into me, like the body of Christ should.

It was beautiful. But that, too, is a tough line to walk when it comes to gauging fruitfulness. Because eventually, you start hashing out the same things over and over, jogging a mental loop that exhausts in every possible way. You start to wonder how healthy it is to repeatedly relive the whole thing. At some point, you have to quit talking and live.

Be.

Pray.

I remember when I reached that point. The day I felt disgusted with myself and how needy I'd become. I hated how obsessed I'd grown with this season in my life but felt powerless to do anything differently or talk about anything else. I wanted to stop caring so much in general. My reality had become a distorted fantasyland that made no sense. I wanted to stop thinking about it all, but it felt like every moment in my day there was a hard decision to make or a reminder shoved in my face regarding my new normal that felt anything but.

For example, the manufactured house I still lived in had various projects my ex had left undone. Walking into the kitchen every day and seeing patches of bare wall where he'd been sanding drove me crazy. Those patches had been abandoned, too, and they mocked me. Even now, if I think about it long enough, I can still feel the swell of frustration from that silly splotch of missing red paint.

Grief is weird. And that's okay.

I learned to keep my venting to only a select few, not necessarily out of guarding my ex in hopes of reconciliation, but for my own health. It was time to focus on other things. So I grabbed some sandpaper, found the extra paint, and fixed the patches myself.

My dad came over, and we used power tools to finish building the stairs for the back porch.

I bought a hideous end table from a local home goods store, sanded it, and painted it a beautiful turquoise that brought life to my soul.

Then I realized my bedroom was now fully my own, so instead of collapsing in grief over that fact yet again, I bought *more* paint and turned an entire wall turquoise, just because I could.

I didn't know *what* to say anymore, to myself or to others, so I just painted. There was something so therapeutic about transforming the old into new. My heart longed for restoration, and while my marriage wasn't getting a remodel, God provided it for my soul—one blue-green stroke at a time.

My friends were there for me, but I had to reach the decision myself to take a step back and redirect my focus. I could have kept complaining, but I recognized it was doing more harm than good, so I intentionally stopped and did something else.

> **My heart longed for restoration, and God provided it for my soul.**

You'll know when you reach that point. You'll know when it's time to find something life-giving instead.

Today, the color turquoise still gives me life. I'm typing this right now while wearing a turquoise sweatshirt, sitting next to that restored little table. The curtains in my living room are the same shade of blue-green, as are the new business cards I just designed and printed. I've always loved the color, but now, it means something more than just an appealing shade. It reminds me of renewal. Of hope painted over scarred surfaces and bad memories. It reminds me of surrender and taking charge and how sometimes those two opposite things fit perfectly together.

What can your "paint" be? Maybe you aren't interested in giving a room a makeover or restoring furniture. But there's something out there that can be your paint—something that gives you new words to call yourself and can give you time and space to heal as you focus on and work toward a goal while allowing your mind and heart a break from the endless hamster wheel of processing. Perhaps it's taking up a new craft or teaching yourself to play an instrument. It could be learning a new language on a free phone app or baking or starting a garden. Or maybe it's getting to the gym for the first time or going back to school to finish a degree. Whatever you find yourself itching to do, do it from the perspective of peace and freedom. Let it—whatever *it* is—be the break your soul needs. Guard that time with your life—you need it.

And the more creative, the better. There's just something about creating with the Creator—whether it's writing, drawing, painting, cooking, composing, coming up with an organizational plan for your pantry, et cetera—that heals our hearts. God alone is the Creator of life, and we're made in his image. Creating resonates with us. And while we can't make something from nothing like he can, we *do* feel a deep connection when we're making something beautiful. And in doing so, he breathes fresh life into us.

> **There's just something about creating with the Creator that heals our hearts.**

While you're painting or sewing or baking or reading, allow the Voice of Truth to speak that life over you. There are plenty of not-so-helpful voices out there, as we well know—including our own. So while you're in your protected time, refresh your mind with the Word of God. Play an audio-Bible app and listen while you stir or dig or plant. Let the Word wash over you and transform your mind while you're jogging, reading, or playing. God always knows exactly what you need to hear, and his Word provides it in abundance.

And unlike the not-so-helpful voices of our own internal thoughts and some people around us, the Lord gets it right every time.

Chapter 11

Counseling Is Crucial

THERE ARE TYPICALLY TWO CAMPS of people—those who completely despise the thought of a stranger knowing their detailed, personal business, and those who eagerly shout, "Take my money!" at the blissful concept of getting to talk for an hour straight and someone being forced to listen.

Personally, I always thought counseling was for couples whose marriages were already on the rocks, or for people who had lived through a major tragedy. Counseling is absolutely for people in those positions, but it's also just as much for people who are simply living their daily lives. People who are processing things that have been and eyeballing things yet to come. People who think they're completely fine with past events and people who know without a doubt they are not.

People just like you and just like me.

I've lived on both sides of that coin, and I freely beseech you—seek counseling. Seek it before your divorce, if possible, and during the separation process—even if you have to attend alone. I knew one couple who went to marriage counseling once a week, and there were multiple occasions where they didn't speak a single word to each other in the week between until they went back. Yet their marriage is thriving today.

There's obviously no guarantee of that being the case, but it does happen, and it is possible. Counseling has a way of getting to the root of everyone's personal issues that contribute to the tension in the marriage, and it provides a safe space for each party to speak freely. But you can't force a spouse to go. Though sometimes I went with my ex-husband, I mostly went to counseling alone. You can't control the other party, but you can choose to go with a heart bent on healing and doing your part. Whether your spouse does theirs or not isn't your responsibility. And whether you go alone or together, there are many benefits to be had.

Before and during a divorce are great times to see a counselor, but perhaps the most important time is to seek counseling after your divorce. It's truly an invaluable tool you will never regret. Trauma needs addressing, and divorce is trauma regardless of the specific circumstances.

If you were the one left in your marriage, go to counseling. If you were the one who had to leave the marriage, go to counseling. The details don't matter nearly as much as recognizing the injury and giving it the attention it deserves in order for you to fully heal.

> ⋮ **Trauma needs addressing, and divorce**
> ⋮ **is trauma.**

Keep in mind, there are no productive shortcuts when it comes to healing. There's plenty of what I like to call "Band-Aid therapies" that simply numb the symptoms for a brief time while never addressing the true wound. Retail therapy, substance abuse, various addictions, and distractions all provide ample Band-Aids in the moment, but they won't last. Eventually, they loosen and twist and fade and come off in the shower, and then you're back with your untreated original malady. The real work of healing often requires professionals.

If you're like I was early in my divorce, you might be wondering how on earth you can afford counseling. It seems expensive, and it certainly can be. But there are so many clinics and counseling services available, especially through church ministries, that will work on a sliding pay scale or even pro bono if you call and ask. Also, check with your insurance. You might be surprised what they'll cover or partly cover. Whatever your circumstances, don't give up. Pray and ask God to provide for you. It's that important.

If you've exhausted all measures and can't find a professional counselor or a biblical counselor, seek out your pastor or a wise, godly member of your church congregation and express to them your need for processing and for biblical guidance. They should be happy to help if they're able.

And if that still doesn't take you where you need to go, you can always counsel yourself via the Scriptures. Pore over the Word. The Bible tells us that Jesus is the Wonderful Counselor (Isaiah 9:6). We have direct access to all the wisdom, truth, and comfort we need. God uses professionals and leaders to help us, and that is a huge blessing. But if there aren't any available to you, you can still seek wisdom with him. It's going to take concentrated effort and discipline to sit down, dig into the Word, and apply Scripture to your life, but it will be worth the time. Make it official—schedule those times in your calendar like you would if you were seeing a counselor in an office. Find a designated spot to go each time. Make it a weekly practice and journal your progress along the way. I filled up so many journals on my prayers during that season (and notes in the margins of my Bible too!).

I certainly could have survived without counseling, but it wouldn't have been pretty. As it was, I sought several counselors over the years that served their purpose for each season and stage of my journey. Before we divorced, when things were rough and up in the air that last year, my ex and I attended counseling together. The man we saw was wise, the perfect mix (in my opinion) of truth and love. And it was helpful, just not in the way I had hoped. I attended, thinking it would change our situation, that somehow the counselor could make my ex stay, but

I quickly realized that wasn't to be. Instead, it provided me someone to go to after the initial bomb was dropped, someone to process those first shock waves with who already knew the whole story. It was a gift.

> **Jesus is the Wonderful Counselor. We have direct access to all the wisdom, truth, and comfort we need.**

Later, I saw a female counselor who helped me navigate the anger and bitterness I was dealing with and who helped my young daughter process her own feelings through the tragedy.

If you are going through a divorce and have children, please get your child in counseling, even if only for a few sessions. They need it. No matter their age, let them talk to someone neutral, one they can be brutally honest with about their feelings and who can help them express those feelings. The counselor in this season of my life guided my young daughter through art therapy and play therapy—she even had her own dog attend some sessions—and it was so good for my kid.

After that season, I switched to another counselor, one who walked with me through my first unhealthy dating attempts and breakups. There is something so healing about having an unbiased person to dump your innermost thoughts and feelings on, with zero judgment in return, who is trained in psychological studies and has experience helping clients navigate trauma.

And remember—divorce is considered traumatic loss. Any event in your life that left an impact can be considered as such. Don't hold back from getting help because you think someone else has it worse or that your situation doesn't count. It does. Divorce can be as traumatic as death. In many ways, it is a death. Give it the merit it deserves, and don't try to walk it alone.

Eventually, years later, I ended up with a counselor who specialized in EMDR, which was a game changer for me. If you're not familiar,

EMDR stands for Eye Movement Desensitization and Reprocessing, and is, in layman's terms, a form of therapy that helps people heal from emotional distress and various forms of PTSD (post-traumatic stress disorder). I also once naively thought PTSD was something only veterans experienced. But it can occur in anyone with trauma. The beauty of EMDR is that it helps retrain your brain and your memories so the emotional attachment to those memories is less intrusive. Basically, it takes the sting out by helping process your memories into long-term storage versus leaving them hanging out and feeling current.

> **Don't hold back from getting help because you think someone else has it worse or that your situation doesn't count. It does.**

For example, there were times when, years after my divorce, I would have the opportunity to share my testimony with church small groups or at speaking events. Every time I got to a certain part of my divorce story, I would tear up so strongly I wouldn't be able to speak. It was both strange and frustrating to me because in the moment, I wasn't even sad. The memories I was speaking about were several years old, and I wasn't walking around upset about them anymore. I had moved on. But that one specific memory really triggered me for no rational reason and made sharing difficult.

I processed that trigger with my counselor, who explained that the powerful memory was being held in the wrong part of my brain. It was causing a visceral reaction as if the memory was fresh. While my logical side knew the memory was old, my body wasn't responding to that truth. It was as if signals were being crossed. Processing through the art of EMDR "moved" the memory to its proper place in the past, and now I can share without issue.

In the same way, a friend of mine experienced a house fire years ago, and every time she heard sirens afterward, she would go into a near panic attack. Logically, she knew there was no danger, but her body was still reacting to an old threat. After EMDR therapy, she can now hear fire trucks with a very mild, if any, reaction.

EMDR even came in handy a few years after I was remarried. One night, I was sitting on the couch with my new husband, watching an old Tom Cruise movie. In the scene, Tom Cruise made a bad decision that felt very out of character for the story. At first, I was aggravated simply because as a novelist, I understand the importance of characters staying true to themselves, even during a developmental arc. Something about it didn't seem right, and it frustrated me, especially since it was such a popular movie.

But as the movie continued, my aggravation turned deeper and more irrational until I suddenly demanded we turn the movie off. My husband blinked at me a few times, unsure why I was reacting so strongly to such an old film. At first, I didn't know either. As the evening went on, I finally recognized what it was. The decision the character in the movie had made reminded me of a decision my ex once made, one I wasn't aware of until well into our divorce proceedings. It got swept under the bigger issues we were navigating in court, so I never had a chance to process or grieve it properly. Poor Tom Cruise got the brunt of it.

I went back to EMDR, processed the memory, and now I can laugh about it all.

There's nothing magical about EMDR or counseling, but there are many benefits to them and they're worth your investment. Please hear me—science and psychology are not on the opposite side from Christianity. There are many Christian counselors who recognize the science behind how God wired our brains and our bodies. We are the full package—body, mind, and spirit—and all three components are affected in a trauma.

If you're hesitant to try a new therapy because it seems too "out there," do some research first, and then talk to people who have tried it. You might find relief you didn't even fully realize you needed.

While biblical counseling and psychology do fit together and aren't a combination you should be wary of, you *do* want to beware of getting pulled into an overtly worldly mindset while seeking counseling. What you don't want is a counselor trying to simply build your self-esteem by telling you how amazing you are and how your ex doesn't deserve you. Building your pride through surface-level edification might feel good in that hourly session, but it won't help you actually walk through the layers of forgiveness and processing you need to. If a counselor is fueling your anger and propping it up as justified rather than helping you find a way through it, you're doing yourself more harm than good. Use wisdom, even in your pain, and make choices that will benefit the person you're hoping to become in the aftermath of the divorce.

As endless as this season may seem right now, it won't last forever. You *will* eventually be on the other side of this. The choices you make while healing will help determine what that other side looks like.

So, stop and ask yourself this. Do you want to be a person fully healed, who did the work of walking through their issues so they can thrive on the other side? Or do you want to take shortcuts, wallow in various "Band-Aid therapies," and delay the better part of your future?

There are so many decisions surrounding your divorce that are out of your control. But the choice of walking toward healing is 100 percent yours.

Choose wisely.

Chapter 12

Faith Walks in Red High Heels

MY LAWYER WAS A 6'5" Sicilian.

The first time I met with him, I felt the strangest sense of surreality. How could this be happening? How could I actually be sitting across the table from this giant of a man with an equally giant reputation, in need of his services?

My sister went with me and helped me tell my story. I'd had to fire my previous lawyer, who—bless it—was a sweet woman, but one who clearly didn't realize what she was getting into. I needed someone to help me and protect not only me but my daughter, not a grandmotherly type who would pat my hand in sympathy while accepting whatever the other side offered.

Side note: the fact there were even sides in the first place still ripped my heart apart. How did "one flesh" morph into two so quickly?

I was reeling . . . and being stared at by this intimidating suited man didn't help.

But he *did* help. He gave me the cold dose of reality I needed for what I was facing. And he fought for me, with his own form of sympathy, against each obstacle we encountered along the way.

It made me think of a verse in the Old Testament I'd always been intrigued by but never needed personally. "The LORD will fight for you, and you have only to be silent" (Exodus 14:14). That really hit home. Of course, that isn't to say the Lord necessarily takes sides in divorce cases, or even that we can wield Scripture like a magical weapon. It doesn't work that way. For one thing, every divorce is different— every motivation and heart posture of every person involved varies and is also tainted by sin.

But the Lord *is* just. And it helped me immensely to know I could pray and surrender my sin and my heart posture (that was undoubtedly affected by pride, fear, and selfishness) to God for him to work it all out. I could trust that he would fight for me and for my daughter, whether he used the expertise of my lawyer or the wisdom of a judge. He could even turn the tide of my husband's heart and provide a road-to-Damascus moment, if he chose to. And the Lord will fight for you as well. Regardless of all the uncomfortable unknowns, we can trust God to fight for us. We can trust that everything will work the way it is supposed to, for all our individual stories and greater good.

> **Regardless of all the uncomfortable unknowns, we can trust God to fight for us.**

I knew that to the fiber of my soul. Still, I dreaded the looming court date when it would all become official. When this ongoing, seemingly never-ending process would, in fact, end.

End my marriage.

My husband and I had already gone through several sessions to set temporary custody, including one where the judge court ordered us to see a mediator in hopes of wrapping things up more smoothly. At the time, my ex didn't believe he should pay any child support, even though I wasn't financially stable and we still had a house to sell and a daughter who stayed with me the majority of the time. We had several significant issues on the table that we needed to reach an agreement about, and mediators typically have a high rate of success.

I could tell you how that went, but I won't. Needless to say, we were back in court with a big *F* for *Failure* stamped on our foreheads. Thankfully, my 6'5" Sicilian was there to fight for what was fair. That's all I wanted—fair.

But no, really, all I wanted was for this whole nightmare to go away. I think that was when I started trying to hide in plain sight.

You know what I mean—when we shift into guarding our hearts, building walls that no mere man could possibly penetrate. Putting on our "game faces."

Up until this point, I'd been bleeding rather publicly. My personal situation wasn't a secret. I wasn't airing dirty laundry by any means, but I was broken and in need of support. And to obtain that support, I had to be vulnerable. Real. Honest. I had to share with friends and family, my boss, my publishing company, and even my reader base a vague version of what I'd been facing. Why my books were late. Why my blogs were irregular. Why my social media engagement was down and my blood pressure was up.

But all that vulnerability started shutting down and closing up shop within me during this transition season, largely because I could no longer avoid the reality of what was happening. I hadn't exactly been in denial before that point, but I sure had been hoping something would shift. That all of this would be unnecessary. That lawyers and court dates and legal fees would go back to being elements of a foreign world I no longer needed a passport to. That this ending wouldn't be final.

But the ending hadn't shifted. And I had to face the grim reality of what *was*.

Most likely, you've done the same at some point in your divorce journey. Carefully slid a mask into place to show others you're past the pain, to persuade everyone that this is now just an incredibly inconvenient hassle in your life, and how about them Yankees? You hide in plain sight, probably behind a new dress or a fake tan or a body you've abused into submission in the gym, and figure if you can convince everyone else that you're okay, you finally will be. Or you blend into the background and avoid recognition altogether because if they can't see it, you can pretend, for the moment, that the grief doesn't exist.

Because you're over it—over the pain, over the rawness, over the hope that if you bleed long enough, eventually, the person who caused your wound will bring you a bandage.

Then when they don't, you dry up. You grow brittle and determine to stop showing weakness, to tend to your own wounds. You hide them because, like an injured animal, it feels dangerous to be seen. But hiding in plain sight doesn't work. If you haven't realized that yet, let me save you some time and energy. Masking the pain only prolongs the pain, and at the end of the day, you're not fooling anyone.

Especially not yourself.

Facing hard things head-on is always better than attempting to stay rooted in denial. When we ignore the truth of our reality, we're also ignoring the path leading to the other side, the path to healing and freedom. The hard reality won't go away. We have to face what is and open the door to the end of our old dreams. Only when we walk through the door can we discover hope of moving into the new season and finding a new beginning. In my head, I knew I had to open the door and move forward. Still, it was the last thing I wanted.

The dreaded day arrived when it was all going to be final. The negotiations, the big wooden conference tables, the stale coffee, and the suited lawyers were all gathering for one last round to make it official.

Like it or not, I was getting divorced.

The word still rolled foreign on my tongue. Kind of like how when you're reading, the longer you stare at a particular word, the stranger it starts to look. Divorced. Di-vor-ced. And you start to think, *Surely that's misspelled . . . surely that's a mistake.*

My sister went with me to court. We snuck candy in her purse.

And I bought a new pair of red high heels for the occasion, because at the time, nothing else seemed to scream confidence like four-inch stilettos. If I was going to be in the reluctant spotlight, I was going to be *seen*, and I would look confident doing it.

> **When we ignore the truth of our reality, we're also ignoring the path leading to the other side, the path to healing and freedom.**

I would fake it until I made it even if it made my feet cramp and my toes bleed. I would send a clear message: I'm just fine. You did not destroy me or my dreams.

The entire process seemed to take a year and only five minutes all at once. There were other divorcing parties having to be addressed in the same courtroom, so our case wasn't the only one. We had to sit through two others first, one of which involved a risqué videotape scandal.

Once again, the bizarreness of my situation overwhelmed me. How had this environment become my reality? This was the stuff that happened in true-crime documentaries or low-budget TV series, not my life. We were supposed to still be a family. We were supposed to be safe at home together in our double-wide in the country, taking nature walks and visiting Daddy at the fire station and laughing at my poor attempts at cooking.

But the man with the cold expression and brittle gaze sitting across the courtroom had become a stranger. The person who'd walked through life, death, grief, and multiple celebrations with me now sat unmoving on a hard seat, roughly five yards yet five forevers away.

Finally, it was our turn. It was a blur. Our lawyers did all the talking, and then I was shoved through the doorway, ending my life as I'd known it.

Part of me was relieved to have it over with, but there was nothing in me celebrating. It was more akin to attending a funeral. Yet no one wore black or mumbled their quiet respects. Instead, the gavel slammed loud, and the clack of the court reporter's keystrokes echoed like gunshots, punctuating every fatal line spoken.

My marriage was officially over.

People talked and shuffled around as they left the courtroom, moving on with their day. There was no acknowledgment that my world had just shifted into a distinctive *before* and *after*.

Bustling out of the courthouse into the warm springtime Louisiana air felt surreal. Cars passed me on the street as I wobbled back to my sister's car in those red high heels. An airplane flew overhead. The wind teased my hair and birds chirped. Everything was so normal and so incredibly . . . *not*. Life carried on, while mine felt oddly still.

And very hopeless.

I had the consistent thought throughout the entire process that the day was forever marred. Permanently a black mark on the calendar, never to be redeemed. March 25—the day I became a divorcée.

You might have that title of divorcée right now, or it might be coming soon. Maybe you're not sure if it'll ever become your title or not, and the not knowing is as stressful as the label itself. I've been there too. It's all impossibly hard.

If you're in that courtroom season right now, you have all my hugs and sympathy. I wish I could send you a giant fruit basket and a lifetime supply of Hershey bars. (And new shoes in your favorite color!) If you're not in the courtroom yet and are dreading its inevitable coming, you, too, have all my love and support. And if you're past the courtroom process and are now rebuilding your life with uncertainty and trepidation, I see you. Whether your wound is still raw or wrinkled by old scar tissue, I see you.

More importantly, God does too.

Because as sad as it all is and as heartbreaking as it feels right now, it's *not* the final verdict. Trust someone from the other side. God always has the last say, even if a slamming gavel attempts to declare otherwise. No piece of paper or court transcript or legal stamp can overcome God's plan for your life, and he is more than capable of creating good on the other side of the doorway. You are not a plan B. You are very much living in plan A. And you have no idea what is right around the corner. You have no idea what this entire journey has been leading you toward.

> God always has the last say, even if a slamming gavel attempts to declare otherwise.

I don't know the specifics of our new lives either, but I do know this—God is leading us toward hope.

We can trust the one who *does* know it all.

For me, that day in the courtroom was truly the end of my marriage. My story was not going to be like my friend's story, who eventually remarried her ex-husband after spending years divorced and then had more babies with him. No, this chapter in my life was closed, but my story wasn't over. And yours isn't either.

God is already at work even while we sit there in court. He's next to us on that hard bench and behind the scenes, all at the same time. He's presiding over the room. He is the God who is outside of time and government and verdicts. He is the one who opens the door to new, good things. It's never too late for hope. Not just hope that your marriage will be restored later or that you'll get remarried to someone else one day.

I'm talking about a deeper, truer hope. An everlasting, eternal, permanent hope—the kind that comes from believing so fiercely that we are loved and seen by Christ, and that the Lord our Maker is our husband, that no gavel or marital status box could ever possibly define us.

That doesn't mean it is easy to step through a doorway into the unknown. The next pages in our chapter often seem written in invisible ink, don't they? We want the answers rigth away, but 2 Corinthians 4:18 encourages us to "look not to the things that are seen but to the things that are unseen. For the things that are seen are transient, but the things that are unseen are eternal."

Sometimes the things we can see blind us to what's really there. Don't give up hoping for all God has for you—whether that's a new husband or not. Hope for his will in your life with a hope that makes no sense. Reckless, intentional, desperate hope that trusts wildly and passionately. Hope that overflows out of us, like that portrayed in Romans 15:13: "May the God of hope fill you with all joy and peace in believing, so that by the power of the Holy Spirit you may abound in hope."

Abounding. Not just a little bit of hope in him, but abundant hope. And it comes from him alone. Not in court, not in legal paperwork or documents or marriage licenses. Not in what we can see, touch, and hear. Just him. He's the only source of fulfillment. He's the only thing to get us through those courtroom days.

For me, I had no idea that day, sitting in that chilled room, the bench beneath me hard and unyielding (and my heart only pretending to be), that several years later I would be in for a big surprise. I had zero idea God was already piecing together my future . . . the future that, in my limited, hopeless view, had been completely obliterated. Even then, God was working to restore and breathe life into that very day on the calendar.

How so?

Because that exact same date on the calendar, that dark day I thought could never be redeemed . . . is my new husband's birthday.

God is in the details, dear friend. I don't know how that will translate over into your story, but I believe it will. He is so intentional, and nothing—*nothing*—is ever wasted on the journey. He's for you, your broken heart, your broken family . . . and he is the Master Artist of mosaic tile. Hope for the masterpiece that's coming. Put your trust in him to restore your story, and as those calendar pages turn, watch for what he'll do. Don't put a box of expectation around what it might look like, but hope for his goodness.

Wait for it. Expect it.

It's coming.

And maybe you'll get to celebrate with a new pair of shoes.

Chapter 13

Seeking to Heal the Ache

I REMEMBER ONE OF THE evenings early on in our separation, *way* before we were officially divorced, when I went for a little retail therapy. My daughter, barely five, had gone to see her dad for a night, and I was alone and struggling. I hated the fact that my life now had a custody schedule and I was going to miss any time at all with her. I genuinely wanted her to keep a positive relationship with her father for her own good, but as a mama, it was hard to adapt to the change. Even before the separation, I was used to it being mostly just me and her because of her dad's hectic work schedule and his side jobs.

I didn't like being in that trailer alone and felt needy going to my parents' house so often. I was tired of crying or venting to my friends. I was an adult. I had a debit card. So clearly, I was going shopping.

My efforts in Old Navy were a feeble attempt to heal the ache. Something akin to having a toothache you can't stop shoving your tongue against—desperate for something to acknowledge the ache. It still hurts, of course, yet somehow validates the feeling. And in my naivete, I thought buying a new dress to wear to my new full-time job would make a difference.

I stood in the poorly lit dressing room and zipped the back of the strapless, bright green sundress . . . in a size 2. And for a moment, I felt better. I was apparently down several sizes, which was something. But while I might have lost weight, the fact that it was because I forgot to eat out of grief was not good, to say the least.

Nevertheless, as I twisted and turned in the dressing room, admiring the crochet overlay of the sundress and the way the green made me appear slightly tan (truly a miracle!), I felt a very foreign sense of power.

Like maybe I was desirable after all.

Maybe I wouldn't be alone forever.

Maybe I still had something irresistible to offer.

But I had zero idea, standing there under the fluorescent lights, that I was about to head down a dangerous path, one where my need to feel seen, pretty, and worthwhile was about to take over the next season of my life.

Shopping those shelves of brightly colored summer clothes, an innocent enough task, had made several other aches rise. Like someone was turning the lever on a giant jack-in-the-box, my insecurities sprang up suddenly, catching me off guard. I decided that I had to, at all costs, shut down the voice of the jester taunting me (with lies that at the time I didn't recognize were lies!) that I wasn't worthy of love. That I wasn't attractive or appealing because I'd been rejected. That I'd be alone forever and if my husband of nine years didn't want me, who ever would? That I couldn't keep a man.

That I wasn't worth staying for.

If you've gone through or are going through a divorce, you know That Feeling. It's desperation, and it wars against logic and common sense and God's promises. It's the feeling that begs to be drowned out with something—anything—to make you feel better.

That Feeling is a liar and likes to cause a lot of pain. Because That Feeling's number one trick is to sneak up, tap you on the shoulder, and whisper illogical solutions to problems that aren't solvable in our own human strength.

For some of us, That Feeling might highlight the lure of retail therapy. It might cause us to buy that green dress and ten others in the store, racking up credit card debt in a moment of weakness and regretting it the next month when we struggle to pay the minimum balance.

> **If you've gone through or are going through a divorce, you know That Feeling. It's desperation, and it wars against logic and common sense and God's promises.**

For others, That Feeling might suggest you wear the green dress to work and flirt with a coworker, just to see if you can and if he'll respond.

And for still others, That Feeling might tell you to use that size 2 green dress and the way it fits to continue down an unhealthy, consuming road of diet, exercise, and enhancement surgery—to force yourself to look an ideal way so any man would be crazy to leave you ever again.

But it's never that simple. You can't shut up lies by feeding them.

When I was pregnant with my daughter, I attended all the classes the hospital offered, including the ones that featured breathing techniques to endure labor. I faithfully attended, practiced, studied, and prepared. Then when the time came, I experienced incredibly painful back labor so intense I can still vividly remember it now, fourteen years later, and I wince. Back labor didn't play by the rules. There was no rhythm to it, like with regular contractions. There was no pacing to breathe through, no way to apply what I had so diligently learned.

Instead, it was a steady, consistent, never-ending, soul-deep backache that gripped in a miserable vise and refused to let go. And as a fun bonus, it brought waves of nausea along with it. I remember how I just wanted something, *anything*, to make the pain stop. I tried massages. I tried sitting and standing in different positions. I tried pain meds in my IV, which only made me feel dizzy and sicker.

In the hospital that night, I was on a mad journey to heal the ache. And that's exactly what was happening in that store dressing room. I was seeking to heal the ache, and at the time, I was in denial that it couldn't be assuaged with material items, attention, worldly validation, and other fruitless efforts to feel worthy of love.

Because that's all it was. An effort, bound to fail—just like that fabric was destined to eventually fade, wear out, and get thrown away.

The dress worked at first, though, according to the world's shaky standards. For a minute, it gave me the desired boost when I wore it the next day at work. I acquired second glances and the attention I'd secretly wanted. I felt pretty, so in my broken mindset, I felt worthy.

Yuck.

Is this relatable, friend? Searching for a high that fades and then quickly searching for another one because your self-esteem and your pride are so deeply wounded nothing can sustain them? The dress didn't sustain me long either—no surprise. I needed something else to maintain my high.

If you're not careful, that's exactly where you will find yourself—paying admission after admission to a ride you never wanted to jump on in the first place.

Consider this. Do you like spicy foods? I do. The spicier, the better. Give me a bag of crazy hot Popchips or spicy Cheetos, and I'm a happy girl. But I've noticed something—once you try to stop eating them, the burn intensifies. Your mouth only really starts stinging once it's deprived of spice. So you must keep eating the chips to avoid the pain. It's a vicious cycle that will never end until you abruptly put the bag of chips down.

May I encourage you to stop eating the chips? To stop buying the green strapless sundresses?

You know I don't mean literally. Take a moment and think of what your "dress" is. What fills you with a false sense of worth and value? Perhaps it's a different piece of your wardrobe. Or it's facial injections and surgery enhancements. It's the latest technology gadget or the way you flirt with someone who should be off-limits. Maybe it's serial dating, consuming too much alcohol, or taking dangerous risks with your life you never would have before the separation. (I could share my list in that department, but my family might never recover!)

Please hear me—whatever high you're chasing, it will end. Guaranteed. Whatever fad you're falling for, it will cease. And whatever buzz you're trying to maintain, it will stop. So walk away. Put down the credit card, shut the book, turn off the TV. Stop the dangerous flirting. Cancel the appointment. Block that number in your phone that's going to lead you into temptation. Turn your car around.

Instead, wait. Rest. Pray. Surrender to the process. Trust that the Lord is not going to leave you in this place of loneliness and heartache forever. You will make it worse if you try to take it into your own hands.

> **Trust that the Lord is not going to leave you in this place of loneliness and heartache forever.**

Remember Sarai and Hagar in the Bible? God had promised Abram that Sarai would give birth and start an entire generation of God's people through Abram's seed. But Sarai grew impatient. Read what happened.

Now Sarai, Abram's wife, had borne him no children. She had a female Egyptian servant whose name was Hagar. And Sarai said to Abram, "Behold now, the LORD has prevented me from bearing children. Go in to my servant; it may be that I shall obtain children by her." And Abram listened to the voice of Sarai. (Genesis 16:1–2)

Sarai decided God wasn't going to keep his promise. Instead of trusting and waiting, she made her own plan and brought chaos upon her entire household. On top of that, she influenced her husband to go along with it. Her doubt was contagious.

The way we live out our faith while in seasons of trial and periods of doubt affect those around us.

So, after Abram had lived ten years in the land of Canaan, Sarai, Abram's wife, took Hagar the Egyptian, her servant, and gave her to Abram her husband as a wife. And he went in to Hagar, and she conceived. And when she saw that she had conceived, she looked with contempt on her mistress. And Sarai said to Abram, "May the wrong done to me be on you! I gave my servant to your embrace, and when she saw that she had conceived, she looked on me with contempt. May the LORD judge between you and me!" But Abram said to Sarai, "Behold, your servant is in your power; do to her as you please." Then Sarai dealt harshly with her, and she fled from her. (Genesis 16:3–6)

Sarai chose poorly. Nations continue to wage war even today because of that decision. She sought to heal the ache of being infertile by going against God's Word and boundaries and made things so much worse for everyone in the picture—for generations to come.

Your bad decisions in times of divorce will probably not have catastrophic, worldwide consequences. But they absolutely will affect your children, your family members, and everyone watching you and your faith from the sidelines. Will you doubt the goodness of God and try to fix the ache yourself? Or will you trust and obey, believing in the One who is faithful even when your own faith feels weak?

Here's the thing. There are many healthy coping mechanisms, such as indulging in a hot bubble bath or a massage for grief-weary muscles, joining a gym to nab some much-needed endorphins, eating healthier for more energy during this season of hardship, or taking up a new hobby to occupy lonely evenings. Then there's *unhealthy* mechanisms. Those are the ones I'm addressing. The ones that don't nourish your body, mind, and soul but instead glorify things like "girl power," revenge, or any other form of prideful independence. If the coping mechanism is coated in pride or fear, it's unhealthy at its root.

I hate riding in elevators. Sometimes I get claustrophobic, and elevators can trigger mild panic attacks. It's not every elevator and not every time, but if I let my mind go there, it's a horrific experience for me. I told my counselor recently while discussing anxiety that if I distract myself on my phone, scrolling Facebook while riding the elevator, I'm fine. I simply need a distraction. Ta-da! I was proud of myself for thinking to do so and preventing an issue.

Except I was wrong.

She gently explained that distracting myself by scrolling social media to avoid the reality of my environment was only reinforcing the anxiety. I was never going to be free of the phobia if I kept that up. Of course, standing there and allowing the wave of panic to wash fully over me while I rode between floors wasn't healthy either. That, too, reinforced the anxiety and the connection between fear and elevators.

The trick is to apply healthy coping skills to make your body intentionally relax, such as deep breathing. The trick is in breaking the connection between the fear and the event. That's where the long-term solution is eventually found.

So—that ache you feel when you think about your current circumstances and all you lost? That soul-deep, gut-churning, heart-wrenching emotion that seems like it won't ever stop? Don't reinforce it by attempting to silence it with unhealthy mechanisms. It will never be soothed by material possessions, attention, a one-night stand, a new relationship, a self-esteem boosting surgery, or any other method of self-striving you think to concoct. You'll be left worse than when you started. The ache? It'll just be ingrained even deeper than before.

Stop digging your hole and hand the Lord your shovel. He's the Master Gardener, the only one in the entire universe who is able to overcome your pain and betrayal and turn it all into a grand masterpiece.

He's the only one who can till over the broken pieces of your heart and plant new things to grow. What you deem weeds, God names potential. Where you sense death, he breathes life. And from the same vines where you feel only the sharp prick of thorns, he calls forth beautiful blossoms.

Stop seeking to fix the ache yourself, and instead, lean into it as you seek to know the only One who can heal it. Focusing your attention on God, his Word, and the truth he speaks over you is the only way to silence the lies flung your way during this season. You don't need a pep talk or a new dress, you need the voice of the Creator singing over you. But how will you hear him when you're trying to drown out noise with more noise?

Don't be afraid of the ache. Instead, take it to Christ. That's where you'll find true relief.

Also, your bank account will thank you.

Chapter 14

Making Room for the Divine

WHEN GOING THROUGH A DIVORCE or separation, especially one you didn't ask for, it's easy to get into a "do it yourself" mode. Call it a rush of girl power, call it feminism, call it a defense mechanism—whatever it is, it's there, lingering under the surface: the overwhelming need to prove yourself to the spouse who is no longer present to see.

For me, it started with things like mowing my yard. I lived on three acres of land at the time, some of which were wooded in the back, leaving roughly an acre and a little more in the front. How hard could it be? Mind you, the entirety of my mowing experiencing to that date consisted of one time in sixth grade when my dad let me use the push mower on our modest-sized front yard. I happily pushed not-so-straight lines across his deep green pride and joy and was rewarded with two blisters and a slushie. (He also never let me do it again, if you were wondering how good a job I did. That, and the neighbor across the street stood in his own yard with his arms straight up like an air traffic controller, attempting to help me keep straight lines. Bless it.)

But surely, I could mow my front yard by myself now, especially on a riding mower. Right? I was an adult who drove a car. No one was worried about straight lines this time. I could get it done to the best of my ability and be proud.

Unfortunately, my girl-power rush hadn't factored in bugs. Or how deeply the yard dipped at the drainage ditch near the gravel road. Or the jet-spray sewer system. Or how quickly one can bail off a moving mower when a spider leaps off a tree and into one's lap.

Three chopped-up sprinkler heads (oops), one half-mowed yard (I ran out of gas), and one fingernail-clawed thigh later (from the spider-extraction fit), I realized I couldn't, in fact, do it on my own.

Staring at that half-mowed yard drove me nuts for the next several days. It represented, once again, how unfair my situation felt and how horrifically out of my control it remained. Eventually, a friend came and finished the yard for me. Another time, after the riding mower bit the dust for good, another friend came and push-mowed the entire thing for me—for free. (Blessings upon him and his children's children!) These friends and neighbors also had to take my dumpster-sized trash cans to the dump for me, because they obviously wouldn't fit in my two-door car.

Do you have an unmowed yard in your life right now? It might be a literal one, like mine, or it might be proverbial. Your "unmowed yard" might be a different project you can't complete on your own or can't afford to have repaired in your home. Or it's a dream or a business venture you started with your husband, and now you're faced with the unfair choice of finishing it alone or abandoning it altogether.

If you're like me, you might be feeling like a needy, desperate hot mess in the middle of it all, eager to prove yourself yet failing every time you try. It's maddening, isn't it? When going through a divorce, the last thing you want is to feel weaker than you already do. It's adding insult to injury when you can't do something. In these seasons, it feels like we're still trying to prove to our invisible spouses that we can manage without them. That they haven't ruined everything. That we are capable women—hear us roar!

But as our futile efforts pile up, our roar begins to sound more and more like a frustrated whine. Pity party, table of one. I don't know about you, but I didn't even want to RSVP to my own event. Regardless, there I sat that day, gazing at my unmowed yard and dead lawn mower, hating my situation yet unable to get up and move elsewhere.

I think that's exactly where I was frozen as my next novel deadline approached.

Remember that two-book deal I got from my dream publisher shortly after my husband moved out? It was time to write book number two, the one featuring Stella, my divorced heroine . . . and I had nothing. Oh, it had a plot. I knew it was about a divorcée seeking to find beauty from the ashes through art and renovating an abandoned movie theater. I knew her name, and I had the first chunk of the story written, the rest of it loosely planned out. But my writing progress was slow at best, and each day that crept by, I lied to myself. *I'll write tomorrow. I know my deadline is coming, but I'll get it done. It'll be fine. There's still plenty of time.*

In the middle of all that, my incredibly understanding publisher gave me an extension, which helped, but progress slowed to a trickle.

I was intimidated by my own book. In my desire to prove myself, to show something to, well, everyone, I'd made it too big of a story in my head. I was afraid, on a soul-deep level, that I wouldn't be able to do it justice. So I put it off and tried and failed and put it off until I ran out of time.

Sound familiar? Divorce can make even the most organized, punctual person feel completely lost and unmotivated. There's something in your life where that resonates—a different deadline of sorts. Maybe a work project or a big presentation coming up or a birthday party to plan, but you can't wrap your mind around the details of getting it done because of the grief still pounding with every heartbeat. Or perhaps there's something you committed to before your separation, and you have to carry it out, but you're weighed down by the enormous burden and everything feels impossible . . . sort of like wading through a giant pond of syrup, unable to lift one leg after the other in the sticky mire pulling you back.

> **Divorce can make even the most organized, punctual person feel completely lost and unmotivated.**

Staring at my giant desktop calendar that day revealed that the consequences of my procrastination had finally arrived. My book was due the next day, and I wasn't even close to being finished. I took a deep breath, emailed my editor, and requested a few more days. "If I could just have until Monday of next week," I wrote, "I'll definitely get it done this time."

Her response back was immediate and completely understandable. Basically, if the manuscript wasn't in her inbox the next day, she wasn't sure the publisher would keep the contract.

In a nutshell, I was doomed.

And I'd done it to myself.

My editor, bless her, was so encouraging. "Just get it down," she urged. "Even if it's an incredibly rough draft, just get it done and send it to me. We can fix it up during revisions."

So I did the only thing I could do. I was at my day job when this conversation occurred, so I went to my boss's office, gave him a brief explanation of what was going on, and said I needed to take the rest of the day off. He was very supportive, agreed to let me go home, and wished me luck. I called my mom, who was once again my daily childcare, and promised I would come back for my daughter at some point. Then I drove to the nearest gas station, acquired two Monster energy drinks, went home, and called a friend to pray over me.

Finally, I was ready. I pulled up my incomplete manuscript and did the math on how many chapters/words were needed to fulfill the story and my minimum contract obligation. Then I cried. It was impossible—so much worse than I had assumed.

You've been there. In that moment of hopelessness, bound up by what feels like true injustice. *If my husband hadn't left me, I wouldn't be in this situation.* You've thought it. You've believed it. *If my husband hadn't left,* [fill in your blank here].

But you know what else? If my husband hadn't left, this book I was attempting to write would have never even existed.

God is in the business of creating beauty from ashes. That was the exact message, ironically, that I was trying to show with my novel character. And it's true for you too. God is more than capable of turning the greatest injustice, the biggest "it's not fair" that you have in your heart right now, into something amazing.

Will you ask him to?

> **God is more than capable of turning the greatest injustice, the biggest "it's not fair" that you have in your heart right now, into something amazing.**

I crumbled on my living room floor and prayed. Confessed my procrastination. Admitted my inability and my fears and my weaknesses. And told the Lord it wasn't possible with me, but it was with him. If he wanted this book to be published, he was going to have to do it.

Feeling ready to give it a shot, I got up, wiped my eyes (and anointed my computer with oil) and then dove in. *Here goes nothing,* I thought. *And here goes everything.*

Every writer has their own process, but on average, it's relatively common for a writer to get a daily word count from a solitary writing session of anywhere from 500 to 2,000 words. An incredibly good, productive day is considered 4,000 to 5,000 words in most fiction circles, and that's usually in rough draft form. As most fiction novels range in completion from 85,000 to 100,000 words, you can see how writing a novel takes a long time!

I started my marathon session around noon. I wrote, stretched, drank my energy drink, and wrote some more. I ate. I updated my social media platforms to document my word count accomplishments as I went, for the encouragement.

Later in the evening, I got a little delirious from mental and creative exhaustion. I remember sitting at my computer, flapping my arms in the air like a bird to help myself stay awake. But I kept writing. I kept updating Facebook. I drank the second energy drink. (Highly do not recommend two in one day!) At one point, I got up and jogged circles around my living room while eating an ice cream sandwich. (Facepalm.)

But I kept going. I kept writing, and updating, and the cheering on social media urged me on. I honestly don't know that I could have continued if not for the accountability I received through the web. It kept my spirits up and made all the difference.

Finally, at 5:30 a.m., I wrote "The End." Emailed my editor. Got in the shower. And went to work. I'd written for roughly fifteen hours.

I'd written 30,000 words in one night.

Love Arrives in Pieces was published in 2015 and is still what I call the book of my heart. It's not my most successful book according to industry standards and sales figures. But I think it's personally my most successful one yet, because I wrote it with the Lord. It's my miracle story.

In this journey of yours, are you making room for the Divine? Are you pleading for his help? Are you accepting the help he sends?

Are you believing for miracles?

Do you dare to believe you deserve one?

I think back to those moments sitting on the floor before I started writing, eyes squeezed tight as my friend prayed for me . . . to that moment where I smeared oil across the top of my computer monitor—not because I thought it was magical, but because it was a tangible act of surrender. I remember my time of solemn confession, knees pressed into the carpet, and that moment when my prayers turned into trust, and I got up to put feet (well, fingers) to it all.

He was with me. He had a plan for that book, and he saw it through because only he could. And I can legitimately tell this story to the glory of God because I feel so completely removed from it. It happened to me, and yet when I tell it, I marvel as if it were someone else. It was all him.

Are you making way for those moments in your life? Do you believe they're possible? Or are they being crowded out with your own efforts to strive and control? To do it yourself? To prove yourself?

To proverbially mow your own yard?

Surrendering comes back into play here. We can't do this Big Thing on our own. I couldn't finish my book alone or even mow my own yard alone, and I thought at the time that meant I was a failure. It brought feelings of frustration and helplessness and only highlighted my grief.

But when we let the Lord take over, when his strength is made perfect in our weakness (2 Corinthians 12:9), the story only gets better. We don't need to stick it to our exes to prove ourselves. We rely on Christ, and his opinion of us trumps all others—even that of our former spouses.

Maybe you're actually a natural on a lawn mower. Yard maintenance and home repair are exactly in your wheelhouse, and you can't relate to this—or to book writing—at all. But I'd bet that *something* in your life needs to be surrendered that's in the way of God moving right now.

Think about it. Where are you hyper-focusing on your own limitations, rather than focusing on God's amazing capability? Where are you sensing frustration in your spirit? What triggers remind you of being left and stir up anger in your core?

What goals or dreams need to be brought to the altar and given over to the only One who can make anything out of them?

Where is your trust? Is it in him or in your own strength?

> **When we let the Lord take over, when his strength is made perfect in our weakness, the story only gets better.**

Now, get this. I fully anticipated the revisions on that last quarter of the novel to be rough. After all, I wrote it with ice cream sandwich smeared across my face, while on a caffeine high, and fighting sleep with half-closed eyes. But I'd gotten that rough draft in on time, and I'd never felt so much relief in all my life. It was as if a million pounds had been transferred right off my cramped shoulders.

A few weeks later, my editor got the long-awaited revisions to me. I opened the document and slowly scrolled throughout, expecting to see a lot of red marks and comments toward the last quarter of the manuscript. But the end of the story was clean.

Weird.

I went back and read those last 30,000 words more thoroughly, laughing at a couple of parts, and even tearing up over one paragraph toward the end. I immediately emailed my editor and asked her about that paragraph. "Did you add that in? Good call. It's so powerful!"

She emailed back, confused. She hadn't written it.

I had.

Make. Room. For. The. Divine.

In your divorce journey, you might still be stuck on trying to do it all alone, in your own power. You're most likely not under a novel contract, but you have your own list of to-dos and should-dos and can't-dos plaguing you. There's something on your radar, some chore or task or obligation taking up space in your heart that feels impossible to accomplish on your own in the middle of this vast wasteland of grief and betrayal. You're circling and procrastinating, full of disbelief. Full of doubt and afraid to hope.

But if you scoot over, just a little . . . if you make a bit of room . . . you might be blown away by what the Lord can do. God isn't limited by our limits. He isn't bound by the ticking clock or white squares on a daily desk calendar. He isn't intimidated by court dates or legal paperwork or judge's gavels. He's with you, right there in the desert crossing, cupping cool water to your face and commanding wind to blow across your cheeks.

He is so, so good.

Stop trying to do it alone. Whatever *it* is, surrender it. Cover it with oil and tears and ice cream sandwich crumbs and trust him to make something beautiful out of it all. Your hot mess is his canvas of potential. Your weakness only highlights his strength. And your "I can't" could very well be his "I will."

Make room, my friend. You won't be disappointed.

Chapter 15

Please Maintain Control of Your Luggage

I DATED WAY TOO SOON.

And because I wasn't fully healed yet, I dragged my baggage behind me like an overstuffed suitcase. I brought all my insecurities with me, and each time the next relationship ended, I carried it further along, collecting evidence of my greatest fears like passport stamps.

Not exactly the trip we plan to take when we're thirty.

One time, my sister and I were traveling together on a work trip. My rolling suitcase was not cooperating with me at the airport. The wheels would get stuck, the bag would fall off the escalator stair, my handle would jam, or some other manner of drama. We walked past a sign that read: "Please maintain control of your luggage," and my sister side-eyed me, laughing. "You know those signs were written because of people like you, right?"

I wasn't controlling my baggage.

So much of divorce is outside your control. The legal fees. The details of the custody schedule and the community property settlement. The tears and emotions. The empty other side of the bed. All these things get packed into your emotions and stored in your brain as you struggle to move forward. What's put into that baggage isn't under your control. But one thing that *is* fully in your control is how you go into future relationships. You can choose to rush into them and tote around your baggage, or you can choose to get healthy first and go into a fresh relationship as a healed, unencumbered person.

If your emotional suitcase is still full of insecurities or bad self-esteem, you're going to project your luggage onto the next relationship. If you're toting around bitterness or anger toward your ex or you have a backpack stuffed with fear of rejection, more than likely, you're going to create a self-fulfilling prophecy.

> **One thing that *is* fully in your control is how you go into future relationships. You can choose to get healthy first.**

For example, I struggled so much with jealousy when I first tried to date again. My self-worth had taken an understandable hit. I'd been abandoned. All of which made me question what was stopping someone else from leaving me too. Deep down loomed the fear that I wasn't worthy of love. That somehow, my ex spoke for all of mankind, and I'd been found wanting.

I projected that fear into unfairly sizing up and turning every woman I encountered—or that my boyfriend encountered—into competition. I lived in fear that he (whoever he was at the time) would choose her (whoever she was at the time) over me, and I'd be alone again. So to avoid that painful situation, I would compare myself. If I came out less than, I'd immediately go into stealth mode, obsessively monitoring their interactions and whether they were appropriate or threatening. Or, as it happened less frequently, I'd compare myself and determine I was superior, and therefore she wasn't a threat.

Ugh. Not exactly a healthy start to dating again—or to Christian living, for that matter.

Social media is a unique kind of nightmare for someone in a new relationship who is struggling with jealousy. I would (gosh, this is embarrassing) notice whose posts my current boyfriend was liking, or if I saw that a mutual friend of the female variety had posted an attractive selfie, I would immediately check to see if he'd clicked that dreaded like button. If he hadn't, I'd feel a thousand shades of relief and berate myself for being ridiculous. But if he had, I'd usually start a fight and make progress on that whole self-fulfilling prophecy thing.

It was a horrible hamster wheel to live on. I kept thinking if I could just stay ahead of the rejection and find proof that my fears were unmerited, I'd feel better. But all I did was keep unearthing things that seemed to serve as proof of the opposite.

It was an exhausting way to live.

(Please note—the potential red flag of a man in a committed relationship "liking" attractive selfies of other women is a conversation worth having, just not in this chapter!)

Needless to say, I lost control of my luggage quite a few times in my post-divorce dating journey. I don't even know if I'd call it a journey so much as a doomed quest. I was trying to re-create something I wasn't ready for, and because I wasn't ready, it didn't exist yet. I was seeking something I couldn't find.

But there I was, slinging around luggage like an airport attendant. The more I expected someone else to take the burden of insecurity off my hands, the more the suitcases multiplied. Because the burden was actually me. Only the Lord and I could do the work needed to get my heart ready to be healthy, for me to be ready to date again and dive freely into the future he had planned. My boyfriends couldn't fix what was wrong with me internally, and I couldn't stop long enough to do the work because my hands were so full of suitcase handles.

What do you need to let go of today? Which handles are you clinging to, creating destruction in your path? Think about it. Don't gloss over that. Really dig deep and ask yourself what your suitcases are full of. What effect has this separation or divorce had on your self-esteem? Your self-image? Your self-worth?

How heavy does it feel right now?

I wanted to commiserate with you and put into words what I know you're feeling. So while writing this chapter, I sat at my desk for a while, trying to find the right words to create a comparison for divorce, but came up with nothing.

You know what I mean. Words continue to fail me. "Going through a divorce is like . . ." (shrugs). I can't do the analogy justice, and I'm the author of over twenty books. I just know it's truly awful. That feels trite to say and still doesn't sum it up. (You're nodding right now. I can feel it!)

It's not enough that divorce itself is an exhausting, emotional nightmare to walk through. No, it's also a life-changing event that starts a domino effect on things you never could have imagined. Finances. Future relationships. Parenting. The side effects are long reaching and seemingly never-ending.

Divorce is a roller coaster careening off the tracks, and you're not quite sure where the runaway car is going to land. (I'm still trying to find an analogy, can you tell?)

Basically, catchy analogy notwithstanding, we can all agree that divorce sucks. And here's the thing . . . it's supposed to. It wasn't God's original design for marriage. The original plan was quite the opposite. Genesis 2:24 says, "Therefore a man shall leave his father and his mother and hold fast to his wife, and they shall become one flesh."

Now, this doesn't mean that if you're divorced, you're living a second-rate plan B for your life. I don't believe that for a minute. My theology teaches me that our days are ordained before time (Psalm 139:16). Neither your breakup nor mine took God by surprise. When my ex walked out the door that cold February night, God wasn't up in heaven scrambling around to try to find a way to make this situation

Please Maintain Control of Your Luggage

somehow good. He wasn't frantically searching to "Romans 8:28" the whole thing. He already knew the plan.

I just didn't.

Recognizing how much divorce sucks is not a pity party—it's the acknowledgment of truth. Going through a trauma of any sort affects your future, and divorce *is* trauma. If you're anything like me, you needed to hear that again. Don't let anyone dismiss what you've gone through with statistics of how common it is, or "Well that's hard, sure, but at least it's not XYZ."

Minimizing trauma delays healing.

Read that again, and louder for the person in the back. Minimizing trauma delays healing. Putting something off as not that important or not that big a deal when it is only makes the situation worse because you're building on a lie. Denial compounds the pain and stuffs down the grief that will—trust me—eventually demand a release. So do your future self a favor, and deal with the heartache now. Your other option is to deal with it later, after it's multiplied.

> **Minimizing trauma delays healing. Denial compounds the pain.**

Divorce trauma is its own breed. It tends to come with the bonus of a myriad of dangling tentacles, all of which like to stretch out and slap your future across the face. (Oh, maybe that's my analogy—divorce is like a monster jellyfish.)

The agony of divorce affects so many things as you move forward, and the number of times you want to whisper (or shout), "It's not fair," never seem to cease. I hope hearing someone else confirm this fact normalizes your situation. I'm sorry if you have to say, "Me too," right now, but I hope it brings you a measure of comfort to do so. That's my prayer for you, dear reader.

I could write a whole chapter on how divorce affects finances or parenting—or anything really.

But right now, I want to focus on something we often forget—how divorce affects future relationships. And more pointedly, how the way we handle our divorce baggage will determine the success of those future relationships.

I think the reason divorce affects our future relationships so completely is because the breakup affects us so completely. A divorce is a line in time. No matter who initiated what, who did what to whom, or who filed first, there's a permanent, glaring line in the sand of your history. There's *before* you got divorced, and there's *after*. And for many of us, that trauma is entrenched. Even after healing, even at your healthiest, even after you've resisted the urge to rebound date . . . your heart is constantly aware of this line in time. Just as scars are evidence of old wounds, there are milestone moments in our lives that mark us. These milestones have an inevitable impact on who you date, how long you date, and how you feel while you're dating.

Back to our self-fulfilling prophecies. Take someone who is incredibly fearful of being rejected. Because of that fear, they put up walls in their relationships. They distance themselves a little, give their hearts space, keep up their guard, and essentially, slowly push the other person away so the other person feels rejected. The other person then, naturally, ends the relationship. So the person afraid of being rejected essentially got rejected but probably wouldn't have if they hadn't been so afraid of it in the first place.

Operating out of fear never produces good fruit.

I wish I could reach through the pages, grasp your shoulders, stare you straight in the eye, and beg you to hear me. If you're still operating out of fear, you're not ready to date again.

Oh sure, there's always a sense of nervousness involved with trying something new. There's always a mild hesitation when faced with risk. But a heart healed from divorce and ready to get involved in a new relationship is one that's confident, trusts in the Lord, and doesn't need to depend on the new relationship to feel stable, loved, or accepted.

Needy hearts break hearts. And yours has been through enough. Don't do yourself more damage by creating a situation you're not ready for. Divorce is the gift that keeps on giving. One suitcase at a time, like the conveyor belt at the airport baggage claim, piling case upon case on the spinning belt of your heart and whirling them around and around until they're claimed.

⋮ Needy hearts break hearts.

May I challenge you to transfer your claim ticket? I know someone who is eager and capable of handling your baggage for you.

I can't help but think of these verses in the Gospel of Matthew.

> Come to me, all who labor and are heavy laden, and I will give you rest. Take my yoke upon you, and learn from me, for I am gentle and lowly in heart, and you will find rest for your souls. For my yoke is easy, and my burden is light. (11:28–30)

We like to really pile on our burdens. If you're like me (or my teenager), you're the woman who attempts to bring in every grocery bag possible from the trunk of her car in one trip, just to prove she can. But usually those attempts leave us with sore muscles, broken grocery sacks, and canned goods rolling down the driveway.

Sometimes it's better to do the work, slowly and intentionally, rather than rush the process. What are you weighing yourself down with in this season of your divorce journey? Are you trying to put yourself out there too soon? Are you looking for a man to fix what only God can heal? Is that airport sign directed at you too?

Here's the good news. (It'll sound like bad news at first, but stay with me!) You can't maintain control of your luggage. Not on your own.

Many of us are all too familiar with how struggling for control affects our hearts, our mental health, and our relationships. Attempting to take control of your heartache and regrets on your own will only create more—or delay your healing.

You can't carry it all, friend. That's the hard news and the good news, all at once. You can't control your luggage, but God can.

"That's great," you're probably thinking. "But what does that even look like? How do I have him do that?"

It's as easy and as difficult as switching your death grip on your baggage for a death grip on Christ. Bask in the truth of the gospel and in the realization that the Lord's yoke is easy. His commands, his teaching, his laws bring life and rest, not striving and stress. It's an acknowledgment and a surrender to the fact that you and I *don't* have this. We can't control this kind of trauma. We were never meant to try.

> The Lord's yoke is easy. His commands, his teaching, his laws bring life and rest, not striving and stress.

What a relief *not* to be in charge of an unruly set of overpacked suitcases!

You might push back on this. You might be thinking right now, "My suitcases are great. Totally manageable. I'm not struggling to keep them in line at all. They're even cute—they have hot-pink polka dots!"

Letting go of control—or even the illusion of control—can be scary. But when you release that grip and flex your fingers a moment, you'll feel the relief. You'll recognize the freedom and peace that come with holding the Lord's nail-scarred hand rather than gripping your identity in your own fist. Perhaps you've managed to cutesy up your baggage, to hide the bulging side pockets and that tear on the corner where the fabric is pulling away from the zipper. Or you've gotten good at masking your fears and pretending your self-esteem hasn't taken a hit, that your heart is intact and not hanging by a thread.

But eventually, that zipper will fail. Eventually, it'll all come busting out, and odds are, it'll happen right in the middle of your next relationship attempt.

Maintain control of your luggage by turning it over to the Lord. Surrender your lack of control—yep, you first have to admit you don't actually have any!—to Christ. Ask him to guide you through your lingering trauma and to make you healthy in him before you attempt to date again. Ask him to shoulder your burdens as you navigate this next layer of healing. Ask him to carry all your fears and insecurities until you get a little further down the road. He is the expert timekeeper and pacesetter. His arms never weary. He knows exactly when to put each piece of baggage down, inspect it, deal with it, and empty it. His timetable isn't always ours, and that might mean you remain single for longer than you hoped.

But I promise—you, *and* your future relationships, will be grateful you surrendered.

Chapter 16

Forgiveness Is a Process

It's funny how forgiveness is easier in some instances than others. For example, I can forgive my daughter pretty easily. I'm to discipline her when needed, of course, but her grievances don't linger with me after the issue has been dealt with.

Like the time when she was four and Hello Kitty–stamped the wall of our house, and later scribbled crayon all over the fireplace hearth. Or even today, when a teenage mood swing gets the best of her and she verbally lashes out. It's easily forgiven—partly because she's genuinely repentant afterward, and partly because I'm predisposed to forgive her as my daughter.

In that same way, we're predisposed to forgive because we're made in God's image, and as Christians we choose to forgive because Christ forgave.

But forgiveness is a gift that's all too often hard to give. It's also one we're always grateful for when we receive it.

I remember when I was a teenager, I came home one night well after curfew and was an internal wreck. I knew my father, whom I respected and loved, was going to be so upset. I expected grounding, or even worse, that heart-crushing "I'm disappointed in you." My stomach churned the entire way home and the entire time I quietly unlocked the garage door and slipped inside. The hallway leading to my parents' room never felt so long. Of course, they were awake in bed, waiting for me, and I braced for my well-deserved consequences.

But my dad didn't punish me or even speak of his disappointment. He just listened and nodded and told me he felt the Lord prompting him to give me grace that night. That was the end of it.

I'd never been so grateful, and I never broke curfew again.

Sometimes we're afraid to show grace because we think that means the person we need to forgive will just do it again. They'll use it as a "license to sin." But my father's grace didn't tempt me to disobey because maybe I'd get away with it again. Rather, it prompted me to obey all the more.

I'd been given a second chance.

Grace and forgiveness go hand in hand and are a beautiful combo when they work together. But too often, the concept of forgiveness is misconstrued and gets twisted in a way that gives it a bad reputation, especially for those coming through abuse and trauma. That's when extending mercy gets a lot trickier. It's easier to forgive someone who is sorry, who you know operated out of character, and who will most likely not repeat their grievance.

It's a lot harder when it's someone who doesn't even seem repentant.

I used to think forgiveness meant admitting whatever had been done to you was okay. To me, it meant heaving a long-suffering sigh and passive-aggressively announcing, "It's fine," when it wasn't.

I've learned since then that forgiveness doesn't mean condoning. That while grace and forgiveness often go together, forgiveness and boundaries also hold hands. Setting a healthy boundary for yourself doesn't mean you can't forgive too.

Let that sink in for a moment, because it might help unlock the cage you're stuck in. You can forgive while taking steps to ensure the abuse or trauma doesn't repeat itself. You can forgive the person who hurt your heart and yet keep your heart protected from their unhealthy behavior patterns. Just like you can forgive your ex without getting back together with him.

> **You can forgive while taking steps to ensure the abuse or trauma doesn't repeat itself.**

To practice forgiveness, we first must recognize that forgiveness is a command in the Bible meant for our own mental, emotional, and spiritual good. It's not arbitrary—it has purpose. Like a parent often must convince their child to eat their veggies, our heavenly Father knows the good that comes from our extending forgiveness. (Even— maybe especially—when it's hard and feels unnatural!) Just like that broccoli, forgiveness is better for us in the long run despite the temporary unpleasant experience.

Before you skip over the rest of this chapter like I'd have been tempted to do in my divorce season, let me expound. Like you might, I used to wonder how in the world I could forgive someone who pledged before God and man to love me, for better or worse, until death did us part, then bailed and broke every one of those promises.

How could I forgive someone who had put me through the worst emotional pain of my life?

How could I forgive someone who had hurt not only me, but also my family, as deeply as he had?

It's an overwhelming thought, and it should be. It's a huge task. But I'll tell you the secret. Forgiveness is not a one-time arrival at a holy, internal place. Forgiveness is a process.

And just like it takes eating veggies more than once to establish a healthy habit, you'll probably have to do forgive over and over again.

For a long time, I couldn't forgive my ex at all. I didn't want to hold a grudge, but I just didn't know how to go about the process of forgiving. I knew the Bible required it of me as a Christian, but I couldn't grasp why.

Then this perspective helped me see the truth behind the concept.

If the person who wronged you is a fellow believer, Jesus already paid the price for their sin. Just as he died for my sin, he died for their sins. Past, present, and future. In that light, refusing to forgive a fellow Christian who sins against you is essentially saying their sin was so uniquely awful that Christ's sacrifice didn't cover it.

Yikes.

And if they're not a fellow believer, then the punishment for their sin—all their sins, including the one against you—will be dealt with on judgment day in a way far worse than you could ever punish. So in that same vein, if we refuse to forgive a nonbeliever, we're setting ourselves up as final judge and jury over and above the Lord.

Yikes again.

It's sobering, isn't it?

I don't know about you, but thinking of it that way brings me more compassion than anger. It rightly puts me in my place, as I'm so often needing reminders. The Bible clearly tells us vengeance is the Lord's, not ours (Romans 12:19).

There are a lot of references to forgiveness in the Bible, but consider just these for starters.

> If you, O Lord, should mark iniquities,
>   O Lord, who could stand?
> But with you there is forgiveness,
>   that you may be feared.
>   (Psalm 130:3–4)

Who am I to refuse to forgive when God himself has already done so?

In him we have redemption through his blood, the forgiveness
of our trespasses, according to the riches of his grace, which he
lavished upon us. (Ephesians 1:7–8)

Who am I to withhold forgiveness when God has graciously forgiven me?

As far as the east is from the west,
    so far does he remove our transgressions from us.
                                            (Psalm 103:12)

Who am I to hold a grudge when God forgets my own grievous sins?

Forgiveness is a process, one demanded of us in Scripture by the
Lord who knows what we need, who is always after our eternal good
and his own glory. But what does it look like? *How* do we forgive, especially when we can't turn off the negative feelings?

I think it starts with recognizing that forgiveness is a decision. If we
wait on our feelings, we'll never do it. Deep wounds leave deep scars.
Even when the initial healing has begun, it's rare for someone to be able
to look at the person who hurt them so thoroughly and feel like forgiving. Don't put that expectation on yourself. Forgiveness takes time.
This won't be fast, and there's no reason to pretend before it's genuine.

Sometimes the forgiveness process just starts with a simple, honest
prayer of "Lord, I don't want to forgive him, but I *want* to want to.
Help me." Trust the Holy Spirit to take it from there.

Forgiving also looks like redirecting your thoughts. It's actively
choosing to dwell on the goodness of God instead of the depravity
of man. It's intentionally thinking good thoughts instead of negative
ones. Not in a Peter Pan kind of way, but in a genuine, "we have the
mind of Christ" kind of way (1 Corinthians 2:16).

When our thoughts drift into anger and bitterness, we discipline
ourselves through the power of the Holy Spirit to pull them back. The

more time you spend in prayer and in the Word, the more you give the Holy Spirit opportunity to work.

It's a lot harder to stay upset with someone when we're immersing ourselves in Scripture, prayer, worship music, and meditation on the way God has forgiven us.

> **The more time you spend in prayer and in the Word, the more you give the Holy Spirit opportunity to work.**

There are also the sneak attacks to keep in mind. Over time, we think, *Oh wow, I did it! I forgave. I'm genuinely wanting good things for this person now.* Then inevitably, something triggers us back into those ugly pre-forgiveness feelings, and we think we've failed. We had a bad dream about our ex, or we saw a movie that reminded us of them, or we see happy couples out on the town and we get hurt or mad all over again at our circumstances. We assume having those negative feelings spring back up means we didn't forgive after all, and the whole concept is futile. At that point, we're likely to give up even trying and just bask in the bitterness.

Don't fall for that.

I went through that cycle several times. There would be days where I would legitimately hope for good things for my ex, where I clearly saw all the blessings the Lord had given me, where I loved the God-made changes in my heart and was truly grateful for the entire journey.

Then my ex would do something that I felt threatened my floundering security or wasn't best for my daughter or reminded me of my battle with loneliness, and I'd stumble right back. It's okay—that's normal. It doesn't make you a bad Christian. It makes you a real one. It's all part of the process. When you fall back, just pray, admit it, and ask the Holy Spirit to do his thing again. As you continue the cycle, it gets easier and faster to stand back up every time. Don't give up.

Forgiveness is multifaceted, and our various stages of grief also cloud the process. Forgiveness is like peeling back an onion, one layer at a time, and it's usually just as stinky. Think of grief as the knife we must use to pull away the layers and find healing. First, we hurt for the present—for our immediate selves. The pain is real and raw and overwhelming. It's relentless. It's a vise around our hearts and lungs and takes time to ease up.

> **Forgiveness is like peeling back an onion, one layer at a time.**

Next, when we're past that initial stage of shock and grief, we start hurting for our future, hurting for all we desperately want to know but can't. *Will I be alone forever? Will the marriage be restored? What happens next? What will I do?* (This layer will probably feel like the longest one!)

Then, we grieve for the past. The memories of good times slice deep like that knife through our proverbial onion. We ask hard questions about what happened. We slip into a time machine—usually one with a very inaccurate memory finder—and idealize and romanticize all we lost.

Then, if there are children involved in the divorce, the next layer is perhaps the hardest. We tend to repeat the entire process, but this time for them.

I remember feeling really caught off guard at this stage. I thought I'd moved forward and had a solid grasp on my life and hope for my future. I thought I'd forgiven. I thought I'd let go.

Then I would see photos in my daughter's baby book or remember good times we had as a family, and I would fall apart. I would feel the impact the divorce had on her and her security and would grow angry and sad once more. I felt like Humpty Dumpty, sliding off the wall over and over again. No matter how hard I tried to stay up there on the ledge, something unexpected or unavoidable would shove me back down to the ground, and I'd crack.

When my daughter was born, I remember my father leaning over me while I held her, his eyes full of love, and his declaring, "Man, she's got it made." He was referring to how loved and well cared for she was and how my husband and I had set up a safe environment for her. On all fronts, she had it made. I would look back on my separation and subsequent divorce and grieve for how suddenly she didn't.

It was the next layer of onion, and it made my eyes sting.

But with some time and perspective, I came to realize I could forgive at each stage, even as my heart went through the different layers of grief. And even more importantly, I came to see the truth that my daughter *still* had it made. Maybe she didn't have the "ideal" two-parent home with a picket fence. But God was writing her story just as he was writing mine, and he used (and is using) each detail and circumstance to mold and shape her into the godly woman she's becoming, just like he did (and is doing) for me.

Despite all those hearty onion layers, forgiveness *is* possible at each step. But it takes recognizing each stage for what it is, and giving yourself permission to get the rush of varied feelings out of the way. No one "feels like" forgiving someone who has betrayed them when the grief is still so potent. Time is your friend here. Trust me, no one is expecting you to put on your best "Christian Woman" T-shirt and fake it before you're ready. (And if they are, they're being unreasonable and have clearly never walked in your shoes.)

Forgiveness will come during and after each stage along the way. Trust the process. Trust the Lord working in your heart as only he can do.

And eventually that onion odor won't even linger in your kitchen anymore.

Where is your heart with forgiveness today? Are you genuinely able to let go and move forward, wishing your ex or soon-to-be ex good things? Or are you still trapped in the bondage of "it's not fair"? Does your heart laugh with grace or cringe with bitterness? Do you feel like you've completed all the steps once before and are somehow back on the hamster wheel of repetition, having to forgive all over again? Are you still grieving for yourself or your kids?

Wherever you are, recognize the stage for what it is and don't beat yourself up. Pray and ask God to help you to the next step. Remember, sometimes the "want to want to" is all we need. I reckon that to be the mustard seed of forgiveness (Matthew 17:20).

And just as my father leaned over me and gazed upon his newborn granddaughter that day, God looks at you and me with all the love and care of a heavenly Father. He declares the end from the beginning (Isaiah 46:10), and he sings over you (Zephaniah 3:17). He's aware of every detail along the path of your journey to forgive. Every struggle, every effort, is not in vain. He sees and knows and cares. And he's equipping you and helping you through each step of the way.

It's a process. It's not painless.

But it's worth it.

Chapter 17

Invisible Chains

SOMETIMES YOU GET DUMPED, AND nine days later, find yourself in jail.

Not in the way you're thinking.

Post-divorce, I'd been in a ten-month-long relationship that ended rather abruptly. In hindsight, it probably wasn't that sudden—I'd just been in denial for the direction it was going for some time prior. Regardless, the ties of a relationship I'd come to depend on were suddenly severed, and I found myself hanging by a thread. It was one more attempt toward remarriage that didn't pan out. One more "now I have to start over again" sticky note taped on my forehead. (Sidebar: it's never a good sign when you miss the relationship itself more than the person you were in the relationship with.)

There I was again, newly single and tempted to once again make an official reservation for a pity party. I desperately needed to get my mind, emotions, and focus off myself. So at the suggestion of a friend, I signed up for a prison outreach with a local ministry. This was my first time to attend, and I had no idea what to expect visiting women who had been arrested. The only thing to do was square my shoulders, don my "Sometimes Warriors Wear Heels" T-shirt, and dive right into the unknown.

The air was stifling and heavy—downright oppressive—in the prison lobby as my group made our way inside. The spiritual veil waved thin, the silent battle around us nearly audible. People were waiting to see family members and friends, wrangling their kids, listening for their number to be called, and paying at the chipped blue booth for their loved one to have spending money behind bars. It was like stepping into an entirely different world.

And I thought *my* normal had been rocked of late. It was more than humbling.

When the inmates' names were called for my group, the three of us made our way through the metal detector (which I set off because of the button on my jeans, which inflicted as much internal panic as you'd expect in that tense moment) and waited to be given our visitor passes. We assumed we'd all be going to the same area because of the similar charges of our assigned inmates, and I was more than grateful to stick with my ministry leader and friend.

Except my pass was green. And theirs were not.

I was being sent to a different area of the prison.

Have you been there? In that space hovering between reality and your comfort zone, staring down a long corridor? Having zero desire to go back and wanting to press forward but feeling quite intimidated by navigating the hall alone? If you've been through a divorce or a separation, I imagine you know that hallway well.

> **Have you been there? In that space hovering between reality and your comfort zone?**

I had no idea what I was doing. My normal had been shaken upside down and inside out. I'd gotten used to a new comfortable in this relationship, albeit one with a lot of unhealthy elements and attachments—and it had suddenly been ripped away. I mourned the loss of the alleged security the relationship brought more than the loss of the actual companionship. On top of that, being dumped brought my divorce pain right back, creating a powerful but invisible undertow. It felt like everything in me was fighting to stay above water, yet I was sinking fast.

Who was I to try to encourage another woman right now via ministry? What did I even have to offer in my own brokenness? I was a hot mess, and all signs pointed to my staying that way for the foreseeable future. And oh boy, that made me angry. Had I made no progress at all? Was I still that weak?

The breakup had jolted my already floundering confidence, and the lies rang extra loud. *You're too messed up to give advice. You spent the last week crying—who are you to offer hope? You're pathetic. You have no authority here.* But I walked on, shaky with nerves and the fear of the unknown, which is sort of how I'd felt for the previous nine days. And I prayed that somehow, despite my fragile state, the Holy Spirit would use me.

That hallway was long—so long. And so was the next one.

But I kept going.

Because sometimes the only way out is through.

Let that sink in for a moment. When we're in the midst of the hurricane named Divorce (I chose hurricane instead of tornado, because tornados come through quickly, and there's nothing fast about the horrific divorce process), we just want it to be over. We look frantically for shortcuts, for safe houses, for somewhere to stall and hide. But it's as if the hurricane is permanently hovering over us, and the only way to get away from it is to keep going. Eventually, the cloud line breaks, and we step out of the shadows and into sunlight again. But navigating through the torrential wind and rain is not only scary, it's loud. Disorienting. And it threatens to drown us.

This particular breakup occurred years after my divorce and was not even my first one since my husband left. Yet something about this relationship ending triggered me in a way previous breakups hadn't. It felt more final. Like the period on the punctuation mark had been pressed a little harder and darker than necessary. This relationship had been much less of a post-divorce rebound (more on that in other chapters!) and much more intentional—at least on my part. This breakup, despite my recognizing immediately that it was a good thing for everyone involved, sucked away my joy. I didn't want that relationship back, but in that season, its ending was like a slammed door in my face. It represented the end of hope. It all felt so final.

That was the hallway I found myself standing in that day in the prison.

I finally found the green door matching my visitor pass and had to talk myself into opening it. Deep breaths. But when I did, I was facing yet another stairwell. I let out a long sigh. Did it ever end?

Would *any* of this ever end?

I felt myself growing angry now. After all, I hadn't wanted to get divorced. I didn't want to go through another breakup. I really didn't want my ex-boyfriend back, but I didn't want more unknown either. I didn't want to walk another hallway or start a new set of stairs. My legs felt sore from my last journey.

Are you standing in a hallway today, pondering your choice? Searching for a door with something—*anything*—on the other side? Are you like I was, desperately desiring security and commitment, even if it was with the wrong person?

In my brokenness, I was more interested in decorating my bad choices and making them cozy, rather than finding a true haven.

I was living in a cell of my own making.

I created a prison to feel safe.

Are you, too, hiding behind self-made bars, hoping to protect your heart? Are you trapped in a cell to avoid being hurt again, so focused on keeping others from coming in that you don't realize you can't get out?

Are you creating a prison of false security?

That's what I'd been missing all along throughout this divorce journey—security. Marriage provides safety nets and familiar expectations, and those had been ripped from me in my divorce. I'd missed the freedom that came from having boundaries and set lines around me, from knowing I was safe. Some people view boundaries as restricting—I've always viewed them as comforting and assuring. Even as a kid, I was the one encouraging my friends to follow the rules. Not because I was such a good person, but because rules had purpose. They made me feel better. Rules made sense and provided a stable foundation.

Divorce rocks every foundation we ever thought we had, doesn't it?

That night in the parish prison, staring into yet another stairwell, I realized I'd officially abandoned all hope of ever finding my way back to the lobby, so I followed a typed sign and hastily drawn arrow toward the female ward. I finally stepped through the frame into a tiny cubicle area with chairs and phones and heavy plated glass. The lights were dim, the shadows long, the area deserted. Even the guard's desk around the corner sat empty.

I stood and waited. Prayed. Paced. Wondered if I was in the right place, feeling more than awkward. All the doubts flooded back in. But then, above all the clamor, came the Voice of Truth a little louder than all the rest.

I stopped pacing and stared at the floor beneath my shoes as reality hit. In wanting to feel safe and secure again after my divorce, I'd attempted to create security and boundaries for myself via new relationships. I felt safe when I was part of a unit—unfortunately, even when that team was not right and proved detrimental to me. Post-divorce, it's easy to let the desire for safety trump common sense or spiritual discernment.

I'd whipped up my own prison to keep myself protected. But I'd used all the wrong materials. Now I could feel my heart shrinking back, tucking down, desperate for a key to turn so I could lock myself safely away. I was so tired of getting hurt.

But I wasn't safe—I was trapped.

There are so many different types of chains, aren't there? You're probably wearing some right now, while reading this very page. You're chained to hopelessness and despair. Or you're chained to the same old faulty way of thinking in the negative. Maybe the words of your ex play over and over in your head, chaining you to a mindset about yourself that isn't true. You might suspect it's not true, but the words are louder than logic, and so the cycle continues. Cornered. Stuck.

Imprisoned.

I mulled over these truths as I stood there in the empty ward, having come to speak encouragement to another but realizing the Holy Spirit needed to speak it to me first. Those endless hallways had officially led me to a crossroads, and now I had a choice.

I could stay in my self-inflicted prison . . . or I could seek true freedom.

This outreach had provided me an opportunity to get out of myself and potentially help someone else, but God knew all along my heart was still the one requiring assistance. There would be time later for ministry.

I first had to decide if I was going to stay in my chains.

Would I keep on with the same unhealthy cycles of dependence, or would I recognize that the temporary lure of a lackluster relationship wasn't really security after all?

Would I learn from the past ten months, or would I allow the temporary feelings of rejection to dictate my truth—and my future?

What about you? What will you do?

No one ever came to me that evening in the ward. My presence wasn't needed. I eventually made my way back through the labyrinth to my team upstairs. Changed. Somber. I still ached from the breakup and its effects on my fragile heart. But I felt hopeful in a new way for the first time in months. Because I was reminded of the truth that it's possible through Christ to experience freedom even from our darkest prisons—the ones composed of thick bars of regret. Cages formed by ironclad materials like heartache and rejection. Even unforgiveness. Even hopelessness.

> **It's possible through Christ to experience freedom even in our darkest prisons— the ones composed of thick bars of regret.**

Along with King David, we can beg the Lord, "Bring me out of prison, that I may give thanks to your name!" (Psalm 142:7).

Don't forget, God is well-known for his miraculous jailbreaks. Ask the apostles. Ask Peter. Ask Paul. There are three different occasions just in the book of Acts. Do you think he's not capable of breaking you free? Do you not think he loves you enough to make the effort?

Whichever kind of prison you find yourself in, whether made by you or not, the key is the same. Christ alone is the answer. He is the only way to have hope for your future, regardless of whether that future includes marital restoration, singleness, or remarriage. He alone offers purpose and guidance on this path you've found yourself thrust upon, this hallway you didn't want to stand in.

When you pursue the things of God—his plans, purposes, and ways—and trust his timing, those prison bars begin to shake. When you fight lies with the truths of Scripture, when you rally in praise and worship, when you battle for your heart with the redemptive grace of the gospel . . . the walls collapse.

Jesus is the only one who can break down the walls of unforgiveness and free your heart from the chains of bitterness. From the lies you're tempted to believe. From your deepest fears.

How do I know? Because sometimes you get dumped and find yourself in jail—and then discover a liberty you forgot even existed.

Chapter 18

The Difference Between Moving On and Giving Up

ONE OF THE BIGGEST QUESTIONS I had during the season of my separation and divorce was when to move on. It's a question without a clear answer. The specifics of when and what and where are going to vary for everyone. But the lesson I had to learn (and I hope you will too) was this: moving on does not equate to giving up.

By definition, giving up means to stop doing something—to throw up your hands and sit in the same place. So you absolutely can move on with your life, living your current circumstances the best you are able, while still hoping they change. You can move on with what your life looks like now and still pray for your marriage to be restored or for a new relationship. Don't think making a change, be it your address or your finances or your job, means you've given up on your marriage. It doesn't mean you're giving up.

But you also don't have to stay frozen. You can move forward.

When my ex left, I was so sure it was temporary. Leaving the house we'd lived in together for almost five years never even crossed my mind in the beginning. Of course he'd be back, and we'd carry on and make new memories there to replace the months of bad ones. Right?

Wrong. As you know, that didn't happen.

The first year, living in our home alone didn't really bother me. After all, that was the only house my daughter had ever known. That's where I prayed over her nursery while nine months pregnant. That's where she took her first steps and ate her first jar of baby food and decided she loved Nick Jr. That was the house where she pounded down the hall in the middle of the night after a bad dream, where she learned how to talk and make mud pies in the front yard after a summer rain. I had no interest in leaving because even though the definition of "ours" had changed, it was still ours—mine and hers.

God gave me a lot of grace in that double-wide and sustained us for well over a year. Emotionally, I was fine being there that year. I didn't look around and continually grieve. I truly was okay there even in the aftermath of such shock and grief, and it's all due to the grace of God. It was our home.

But when the day came to make a change—to move on—it came abruptly.

⋮ **Moving on does not equate to giving up.**

I don't remember the circumstances or if there even was a specific catalyst. It just happened. All along, finances were a factor—I couldn't afford to stay there on three acres, nor was it practical since I wasn't a farmer. (You've already read about my chaotic attempts to simply mow the yard or take my trash to the dumpster!) It was also somewhat secluded. I didn't feel safe out there alone in the night.

The bottom line was that acreage had been my husband's dream, and he'd abandoned it.

It was time for a new dream. And it was time now.

You might have your own account of something similar. Being stuck in the same place of betrayal and sadness can feel overwhelming. Maybe you were ready to move on from the first day you realized your divorce was actually happening. Or maybe you were okay for a season and were able to ease into your new life gradually, like I was. If you haven't gotten to that point yet, you'll know when it's time.

I was finally—after a borderline comedic series of obstacles—able to sell the manufactured house and land and make a fresh start. (Have you ever sold a used trailer? It's tough.) I ended up in an adorable apartment complex with security, alarms, and a pool that turned out to be another grace of God. I don't know how many evenings my daughter and I spent in that oasis, eating five-dollar take-out pizzas, reading, splashing, and making desperately needed new memories.

I couldn't afford movers at the time, so my grandparents generously hired the muscle we needed to get us transitioned. Of course, it was summer in Louisiana and I had to get an upper floor apartment. I still remember those burly movers dripping sweat across the faux hardwood floors of my apartment as they wrestled my bed frame into the master bedroom. (Sorry, guys!) I provided donuts and my eternal gratitude to everyone else in my family who stopped by to help me lug boxes, unpack, and get pictures hung on the wall. Everyone subconsciously seemed to understand my core-deep need to nest immediately, and we had my place completely put together in a single weekend. So much grace.

The weirdest part for me was, I'd never lived alone before. I had gone straight from my parents' home, the house I'd lived in since third grade, to my first home with my ex-husband, to that double-wide out in the country. I'd never even had the college dorm experience or roomed with a friend.

Technically, I still wasn't living alone because I had my kiddo, and we'd lived alone in the country for over a year before moving to the apartment. But it was an entirely different experience, picking out my own place and being solely responsible for paying all the bills, locking doors, setting alarms, and calling maintenance. I was an adult, but doing it alone felt like Adulting 2.0.

We all have those gaps and scary holes we're suddenly required to fill. Looking back, though, we can easily see we weren't as alone as we first felt.

For me, my maintenance man was a godsend. And I kept him busy (facepalm). I remember working on a deadline one day, sitting at my writing desk in the dining room turned office space, and spotting motion from the corner of my eye—white suds, flowing out of the dishwasher. I also went through two garbage disposals (oops). And that first week I moved in, I threw away a rotted watermelon which made the trash bag so heavy I couldn't even pull it out of my trash can without the bag ripping, so that kind gentleman toted it away on his golf cart. (I couldn't make this stuff up!)

So many people, so many blessings to welcome me into this new season in my life. Such kindness shown to me, all by people who will probably never read this book or realize the impact they had on a hurting single mama.

For example, the neighbors who lived across the stairs from us— the young newlywed couple who had no problem exchanging notes with my little girl on our front doors. During the holidays, we'd tape candy canes on theirs, only to find a Little Debbie Christmas tree snack taped to ours.

And the single dad who lived below us—he had no complaints about my daughter stomping around and was only grateful we couldn't hear how noisy his own kids were. One night, coming home to our apartment, I somehow managed to lock my purse, phone, everything, inside the car. My daughter and I stood outside, peering into the tinted windows, completely helpless. Even the medicine she needed was stuck inside that yellow Camaro. There was nothing to do but knock on his door and ask to use the phone. My kiddo watched TV while he and I sat at the kitchen barstools and I called Pop-A-Lock. We chuckled at how our apartments were the inverse of each other's while I tried not to feel like a complete failure of a mom. I'm so grateful he let me use his phone and gave us a safe place to wait.

My daughter and I were bummed when the newlyweds moved out, but the single mom who moved in became a fast friend. She knew from my social media account how much I liked peanut butter, so one day I came home to a giant jar on my doormat. We helped each other out and watched each other's backs. We're still connected today.

There were *so* many hard things at this stage, but there were some fun perks too. I got to decorate (and girlie up!) the apartment any way I wanted. Of course my daughter's bathroom was nothing but trendy Target owls and pink footstools. The kitchen boasted a custom photo-printed *Gilmore Girls* decorative plate, and my holiday decorations that first year were everything hot pink, purple, turquoise, and glitter. I was free to do anything I wanted.

But there was still the odd realization every time I came home that everything was exactly the way I'd left it. There were no more steel-toed boots by the front door, no work jackets hanging in the foyer, no fire department uniforms in the laundry hamper. The food in the fridge was exactly what I'd purchased. The trash didn't get taken out unless I took it. The thermostat didn't change unless I changed it.

Moving on is a long season of transition.

If you're in that season now, I'm sorry. It can be rough. But don't give up. There are so many gifts! And you're not alone.

Fred Rogers, better known as Mr. Rogers, is credited with a quote that I believe really resonates here. "When I was a boy and I would see scary things in the news, my mother would say to me, 'Look for the helpers. You will always find people who are helping.'"[1]

There are always helpers. Like that cute newlywed couple with their Christmas tree cakes, and the single dad, and my peanut-butter-supplier neighbor. The patient maintenance man. Even the elderly Pop-A-Lock worker who unlocked my car. I was borderline teary and berating myself for making such a big mistake. But he looked me straight in the eyes and told me I was a great mama. Sometimes I still wonder if he was an angel.

When you're going through a tough season like divorce, your bandwidth seems permanently shrunken. Instead of operating at a manageable two on a stress-level scale of one to ten, you're operating at a continual seven. Then when something truly stressful happens, it doesn't take much to reach your full capacity of ten. I felt like that's how I stayed for years—a perpetual stress-level seven. But the generosity and kindness of my neighbors and the strangers I encountered during that season helped regulate me back down to a manageable level.

I had helpers. And you have them too. Maybe yours don't bring peanut butter or offer cell phones or tote watermelons away for free, but they're there. It could be the nice day care worker or the mothers-day-out staff taking care of your kids. Or it's that neighbor down the street who brings your cans up for you after trash day or the mailman who always has a big smile. It's the store clerk who went out of his way to help you, not knowing you were having a bad day, or your boss who showed you grace and patience you didn't deserve.

Whether it feels like it or not, people do care. It's hard to notice because you're focused on how the one person you want to care—your ex—doesn't seem to anymore.

It can be so hard to know when to move on, when to accept the reality of what's happening around you and take the tangible steps to care for yourself. Because unfortunately, life doesn't stop for divorce. Creditors still expect payments. Employers still expect hours. Kids still expect chicken nuggets. You're in the midst of trauma, and you still have to pay the bills and water the flowers. It doesn't seem fair, but it is reality.

And I really believe there's grace in that too. Taking care of business, creating routines, and establishing a new normal are healthy ways of dealing with your reality, emotional as it may be along the way.

Regardless of the timing of when or if you decide to move on, God uses our community around us to help us not give up. Remember, we can move on without admitting defeat in our marriage. If you're still feeling led to pray for your marriage to be restored, you can do that just as effectively from the home you once shared with your husband as you can in a new place that's all your own.

> **Remember, we can move on without admitting defeat in our marriage.**

The crucial factor is to do what brings you peace. Is it more peaceful to stay in the memories where you're at, or to go where you can form new ones? You're the only person who can answer that.

On the flip side, you might be stuck and don't have the option to change your living arrangements, but you desperately wish you could. In that case, do what you can to personalize things in your space and give it a fresh look. Switch out the throw pillows on the couch. Paint a wall. Rearrange the furniture. Change out the decorative art. There's a lot of little, affordable things that would help your space feel more like you in this transition and less like "us." That's an important distinction for your children too. If you're staying in your home for the time being, I wouldn't advise you change everything. Rather, tweak it to bring you the change you need while keeping the familiarity and comfort that they might still need.

I remember that first or second Christmas in my new apartment, when my young daughter and I were trying to put up the Christmas tree. The pre-lit lights were partially burned out, and I was frustrated with the entire scratchy thing. I made a comment about getting a new tree for the next season, and my daughter's eyes widened. "No," she whispered urgently. "The new tree won't know anything."

Needless to say I waited a few years!

I speak to single moms a lot in this book, because that was my experience and because, statistically, there are so many of us out there. But maybe you're not a single mama. Maybe you have grown children or no kids at all, and going through a divorce means you're now in a unique kind of lonely. That's hard. Community is going to be vital. You're not meant to walk this alone, and you shouldn't try. In fact, you might be surprised at how many other women are in your shoes right now. They're out there, and they're looking for someone to connect and cry with too.

> **⋮ You're not meant to walk this alone.**

Or perhaps you had to leave your home immediately because it wasn't safe for you to stay. If that's the case—first, I'm so sorry, and second, you did the right thing. It's never good to stay in a marriage where your safety is threatened. If you've experienced abuse at the hands of your spouse, I weep for you and am here with all the hugs and prayers. You've taken hard steps to get away and be safe, and you're probably dealing with backlash from people who don't understand the full situation.

If that is your circumstance, and you had to rush to physically move on and move out from the very beginning, you're in a different transition. You didn't take a slow wade into the pool—you were pushed straight into the deep end. Maybe you even had to leave things behind that were important to you.

If that's you, you can still make the most of this transition season. You can still make your new home, whether it's an apartment, a house, or a family member's spare bedroom, into your own space.

There are still helpers.

There is still hope.

Whether you had to leave or were left . . . whether you moved out or stayed put . . . know this. You are not, and will never be, alone. Kids or no kids, pets or no pets, you're not on your own. Consider this verse from the book of Psalms.

Where shall I go from your Spirit?
Or where shall I flee from your presence?
If I ascend to heaven, you are there!
If I make my bed in Sheol, you are there!
If I take the wings of the morning
and dwell in the uttermost parts of the sea,
even there your hand shall lead me,
and your right hand shall hold me.

(Psalm 139:7–10)

I knew when it was time for me to move out, and I knew when it was time for me to move on. Those two events aren't always simultaneous. Whatever stage you're at right now, it's okay. I see you—and more importantly, so does the Lord. He's with you, right now, wherever you are. If you're a believer, then he'll never leave you, no matter what happened in your marriage. You can't escape his presence, whether you move into a new home or stay in your old one.

He's the greatest helper we could ever hope for.

And he'll never move on without you.

Chapter 19

Attention: You're Still Married

THERE WAS A LOT ABOUT getting an unwanted divorce that surprised me. Like the price tag of a good lawyer, the myriad vocal opinions from people around me, and the insecurities that flared for years afterward with no rhyme or reason.

But the one thing I didn't fully grasp, despite having seen others walk through it from a distance, was how *long* the entire process took.

Despite popular opinion, divorce isn't simply a breakup. It's an *untangling*. It's the knotted gold chain on your favorite necklace that you spend hours hunched over with a straight pin and tweezers, trying to work out the kinks. It's the knot in your shoelaces that you tied too tight and now you wonder if you're going to have to use scissors to cut them free. It's the rat's nest on the back of your head that somehow embedded itself in your hair while you were sleeping, and nothing short of a salon treatment can save you now.

Divorce is messy. It's uncomfortable. It's frustrating. It *hurts*.

And it's so drawn out.

When you break up from a dating relationship, you can often handle the entire situation with a single phone call or text message. (Don't do that, though. That's tacky.) Worst case, an uncomfortable face-to-face conversation takes place, and then the deed is done. You don't have to talk to each other ever again if you don't want to.

One of my relationships that I had post-divorce ended that exact way. He came over and said what he needed to say. I nodded a lot and then showed him to the door, and that was it. I literally haven't seen, spoken to, or heard from him again, even in passing, since that very moment.

Pretty sure it was the cleanest breakup in the history of breakups.

But marriage isn't that simple, and it shouldn't be. Marriage is not extreme dating, despite popular opinion. Undoing two tangled-up lives and all that comes with that takes a long time, and mine took even longer than it needed to.

Allow me to tell you a tale.

Once upon a time, a young man proposed to a young woman on a dinner cruise in New Orleans. They set the date for August and followed all the traditional steps—planning the wedding colors, searching out a place to live, attending premarital counseling. And when they went to the courthouse for a marriage license, they took one not-so-traditional step and chose to have a covenant marriage. They were married five months later at ages nineteen and twenty, never assuming at the time how strongly that one decision would affect their lives a decade later.

That was me and my ex-husband.

If you're not familiar with the concept, a covenant marriage in Louisiana means that you can't legally get divorced without forced religious or professional counseling beforehand. It also drags the divorcing timeline out from a standard six months (with no kids involved) or one year (if there are kids involved) to *two* years.

You're probably thinking, *Good gravy, why would anyone ever do that on purpose?* Well, when you're two Southern Baptist kids who grew up in the era of purity rings and "True Love Waits" pledge cards, you mistakenly think a covenant marriage translates into "extra holy" or "super Christian."

Looking back, I realize how unnecessary that step was. All marriage is a covenant before God. It's all holy. I didn't need the state of Louisiana to agree to make that true. Of course, I never could have predicted how that one paperwork detail would kick me later either.

In theory (and in a perfect world) a covenant marriage is a nice idea. It makes the act of divorcing harder, which in some situations can be a good thing. Some marriages can be restored by enforcing that both parties will take time to reconsider. A covenant marriage prevents hasty mistakes and emotion-led decisions. It insists on counseling, where many couples have success in airing out their grievances and striking a compromise for the future.

But when one party's mind is already made up, and there is no restoration to be had, a covenant marriage only adds pain to an already unbearable situation.

Don't get me wrong. Ending a dating relationship can also be painful and messy. There can be awkward exchanges of possessions after the fact, unwanted run-ins at the gym or your favorite restaurant, and uncomfortable memories that hit when you hear your song on the radio. Depending on how long you were together, it can be incredibly difficult to break up. I well remember how the relationships that I had to end (or that were ended for me) while dating post-divorce were not pain-free for either party. (Or even drama-free on some occasions!)

But even then, in those hard situations, my heart remained intact.

Remember the ripped paper analogy? Divorce is separating what was spiritually one flesh.

Taking two lives and blending them into one—one household, one bathroom, one joint checking account—is tricky enough. But taking that blended life and trying to create two separate ones again is never easy or clean. Just like you can't separate the strawberries and bananas from your smoothie after pureeing them together, two becoming one was never meant to be undone.

> **Taking two lives and blending them into one is tricky enough. But taking that blended life and trying to create two separate ones again is never easy or clean.**

There's also a deeper level of trust you have with a spouse that doesn't typically transfer over into dating relationships. I hope you trust the person you're dating on some level, or you should probably not be dating them. But when you're dating, you don't have the same security of "for better or for worse" and "till death do us part" like you do (or at least should) when you're married. When you're dating, everything is still shiny and best foot forward. It's authentic, but it's not the whole package yet. There's something so reassuring and trustworthy about someone who has seen you at your worst—appearance-wise, attitude-wise, and beyond—and still wants to sleep in the same room at night and brush their teeth beside you in the morning. Someone who has held your hair when you're sick and knows how much of that hair you shed on the bathroom floor and doesn't care if you're wearing makeup while watching TV late at night. There's no pretense. Marriage is just different in that way.

Now, couples who live together before marriage or even participate in common-law marriage might think it's the same as what they have, but it's not. There's not a biblical union in those instances, and there's no weight of glory that comes along with it. It's an imitation of the real thing because it's not steeped in covenant. (And I mean true biblical covenant, not the Louisiana version!)

Marriage carries a spiritual component that dating and even en-gagement don't have. I don't mean to diminish the pain of a bad dat-ing breakup—that's legit. Rather, I'm emphasizing the gravity that a broken *covenant* carries. And that's because of what marriage really is—a reflection of our relationship with Jesus.

Check out what Isaiah 62:5 says: "For as a young man marries a young woman, so shall your sons marry you, and as the bridegroom rejoices over the bride, so shall your God rejoice over you."

Earthly marriage is a picture of the covenant between Christ and his church. We are the bride of Christ, and he is the Bridegroom. Earthly marriage is but a shadow and a type of the real thing we've yet to experience in heaven. When we've passed from this earth, be it from death or from the imminent return of Christ, we will not be married in heaven to anyone but God (Matthew 22:30).

Theologians believe, from multiple Scripture references, that spouses will know each other in heaven but the relationship will look different than it does here on earth. For couples in thriving marriages today, that might make them feel a little sad. But we are assured that we won't feel that way in glory. Revelation 21:4 says, "He will wipe away every tear from their eyes, and death shall be no more, neither shall there be mourning, nor crying, nor pain anymore, for the former things have passed away."

For those going through a divorce or dealing with unwanted single-ness, this is great news. One day, all relationship drama will be over, forever and ever, amen! No more insecurity, uncertainty, trust issues, legal fees, betrayal, pain, custody battles, or heartache. One day, all will be made right, and that dull ache of incompletion we feel deep in our hearts will be fully satisfied in the presence of the Lord. What a day that will be!

But in the meantime, there is hope here on earth too. Healthy, godly marriages do exist. I know you're eager to find it, but I urge you, if you're not officially divorced yet, don't try to date. I know it's tempting to do so anyway, and you might have to learn that lesson the hard way (as I did), but if you have ears to hear, please hear me.

Wait.

I know the divorce process can seem endless and so do those lonely nights alone in a king-size bed, but please wait. If you're not legally free of the marriage, your heart and head aren't free either. You might feel like you are, but there's a subconscious awareness deep inside that will project into your circumstances, like it or not. If you try to date too soon, you'll probably only attract other people who also aren't completely healthy or ready. It's just not worth it.

Waiting six months, a year, or even two years can seem impossible. I know it felt incredibly overwhelming for me. I recognized well before the end of our timeline that the marriage was over. My husband wasn't coming back. It was done. I thought, *I don't need the state of Louisiana to agree on this to make it true.* The process felt so futile and unnecessary, waiting for paperwork to clear when our covenant before the Lord had already been broken.

But looking back, I wish I'd been a little more patient and not rushed into dating before my legal time frame was up. I wish I had recognized that I was still married until I wasn't. I could have saved myself a lot of hurt, drama, and confusion. Thankfully, I know the Lord works all of that to my good and for his glory, just like he's working in your mistakes. Remember, you won't walk this perfectly.

A divorce is not just a breakup. But that doesn't mean you can't become whole again on the other side. The effects of the "ripped paper" or the "blended smoothie" can be healed. You're not permanently or irreparably damaged.

Healing is always possible because all things are possible with Christ.

Isaiah 53:5 says, "But he was pierced for our transgressions; he was crushed for our iniquities; upon him was the chastisement that brought us peace, and with his wounds we are healed."

You can be made whole because of who he is. Not because of your marriage status. Not because you're finally ready to start dating again or because you finally got remarried. When we turn our hearts and attention to that cross, we're no longer dependent on a relationship to fulfill us. We realize our identity is not in anything we do or say, but in who Christ is. At that point we can date, or not. Get remarried, or not. There's glorious freedom to be held when we realize that we're already whole, bare ring finger and all.

> **You can be made whole because of who Christ is. Not because of your marriage status.**

Our marital status doesn't define us. Divorce doesn't forever label us. We're covered by the blood of Jesus, not by a scarlet letter of shame.

We're the bride of Christ. In the grand scheme of things, our hearts are already taken. Without that perspective shift, it's a difficult road. We can still pursue godly marriage this side of heaven, but when we make it the be-all and end-all of our identity and worth, we're setting ourselves—and any future relationship—up for failure.

Wherever you are on the journey, may I encourage you to pause? To look up. And ask the Lord for a fresh view of how he's working in your life, even in this very moment. Because he absolutely is.

As endless as this path appears, it does end. There is another side. The divorce process can often seem like it's taking forever, but this weight you feel right now won't last. There is an end in sight—legally and emotionally. You can be free.

Yes, divorce hurts and brings consequences that tend to last far longer than we anticipated. Yes, there are things to tend to, legally and otherwise, that we can't ignore. Yes, the ache of grief and loss we feel so deeply is real and should be dealt with.

But God is perfectly capable of untangling all those messy threads and smoothing out your weary heart.

Maybe it's time to set down your efforts and all your striving with tweezers and straight pins and surrender the painful knots to his care. This isn't something to work out alone. He's much better at it, trust me. His hands are steadier, his eyesight sharper. He knows exactly what your heart needs, which threads are a little rawer than the others, and which ones could stand some gentle tugging. He's working, even now, to put your heart back together.

This is *not* just a breakup. But it's also not unmendable when you submit to the nail-scarred hands of the Great Physician.

He's here in your pain, working to fix what's broken and to restore all that was lost. And no matter what earthly relationships you might or might not have further down the road, you are always safe and secure in your covenant with him.

As the bride of Christ.

And that is one marriage vow that will never, ever be broken.

Chapter 20

Do It Scared

GOING THROUGH A DIVORCE HAS a way of forcing you out of your comfort zone. There are so many things you have to do but don't want to do. Things like living alone, attending court hearings, taking over your own finances, getting a full-time job or a side job, changing churches or groups (where you were always known as a couple), raising a child by yourself. You now have to be the resident insect killer, the one to check the house late at night when you hear a weird noise, and the smart one to figure out how to change the batteries in the screeching smoke detector at midnight.

You have your own list. You know.

As you take care of the list, there are other items that tend to slip off your radar because your energy is being poured into the non-negotiables. Unfortunately, friendship can be one of those things that slide through the cracks—and all too often, the enemy of our souls makes it even easier by telling us lies about the people who care for us.

When you're going through a divorce, there's such temptation to withdraw from your existing friends. You don't necessarily want to talk about what's happening, but since that's all you can think about, you go into hermit mode to avoid having to consciously suppress your thoughts and words while around others. Or maybe in those initial weeks of separation, you lost your appetite, so going out for a drink or dinner simply doesn't sound appealing.

At first, that urge to withdraw stems partly from the whole "why is the earth still spinning?" disconnect we feel when going through a time of intense grief. Our world is in shock. How could anyone eat chips and salsa at a time like this? That's understandable.

> **How could anyone eat chips and salsa at a time like this?**

But after some time passes, the desire to withdraw is less about disorientation and more about extreme protection—of yourself, your ex, and even your friends. You don't know what's going on in your marriage or what's going to happen next, and you don't want to bad-mouth your spouse in front of your mutual friends, so you stay away. Or perhaps there's a sense of doubt when you're around them, and you're afraid they might be judging you or him or both of you. I remember feeling wary at first and hating that this situation made my friends feel uncomfortable too.

When my ex first moved out, he went to stay with a guy who had been a mutual friend of ours. Of course, they were closer, but I technically knew the friend first and had a connection as well. It felt like the worst betrayal for him to house my husband those first few months. From my perspective, he was helping my husband leave me. But from my friend's perspective, he was giving his friend a safe place to go while sorting things out. In hindsight, I can recognize the tough spot he was in and can appreciate it.

There are always two sides.

It's incredibly easy to get paranoid and project our feelings and assumptions onto our friends. But as we well know, feelings aren't always truth. Sometimes, especially in seasons of grief or shock, our instincts are off and we don't filter properly. In the spinning of our world, we end up misreading and second-guessing. Add in the spiritual warfare element of the enemy trying to keep us isolated from Christian fellowship, and it's a *lot* to navigate. But in most cases, our friends are simply trying to figure out how to be there for us and are as confused as we are. They hate it, too, and are fighting their own battle in determining what we need and how they should act.

But try to resist the urge to withdraw completely. You need them, and here's the thing—they need you. From their perspective, their friendship with you didn't change because your marriage did. If you push them away, they're losing a friend while you're losing a marriage. You might not be able to control your spouse, but you don't have to compound your loss by losing another person you love. Let your friends serve you.

And the important thing to remember with that is communication. *Tell* your friends what you need from them. If you need a week of silence, tell them. If you need them to blow up your phone with supportive texts and be content that you don't write them back, tell them. If you want them to come over and sit quietly, tell them. If you want them to come over and distract you with joke books and sushi, tell them. If you don't know what you need and just need them to keep trying, tell them. They can't read your mind and are probably desperate for instruction about how to best serve you in your storm.

Don't believe me? Think about it in reverse—if they were going through unwanted divorce, would you bail on them? Would you judge them and feel awkward and leave them all alone to figure it out? Of course not. So don't assume they want to do that to you. They need some guidance.

I remember in those first months of separation how my friends rallied around me—even the ones who were long-distance. My phone, my email inbox, and my physical mailbox were flooded with messages of support and love as word began to get out. One friend from Alaska sent me a card with a sweet message and this verse handwritten on the back: "The LORD your God is in your midst, a mighty one who will save; he will rejoice over you with gladness; he will quiet you by his love; he will exult over you with loud singing" (Zephaniah 3:17). I still have it, and it's in my box of Things Most Likely to Be Grabbed in a Fire.

> **"The LORD your God is in your midst, a mighty one who will save."**

So many others were there for me in intentional, creative ways. Reminding me they were praying for me. Sometimes praying out loud for me right then and there. Checking in for regular updates. Sending funny memes and heartfelt texts. Distracting me when I needed it, crying with me when I didn't want a distraction. I knew my name was being scribbled in countless prayer journals across the country. I could depend on my friends, and that realization brings tears to my eyes even now. We might have been separated by the miles, but we were connected in spirit. I was gaining numerous valuable treasures even as I was losing so much.

I hope you have this in your life. I hope you're clinging to your friendships in your time of heartache and allowing them to pour into you. But if you don't have people, if your life was hectic and your friendships sporadic leading up to your separation, then you need this next piece of advice even more.

(And I'm fully aware it sounds a little ridiculous and borderline impossible, but it's also one of the best decisions I ever made.)

Take this season as an opportunity to make new friends.

Say what, now?

I know. It doesn't make sense on the surface. You have plenty happening at the moment, right? The last thing you want to do is put yourself out there, to be the new kid at the lunch table trying to trade snacks. But trust me—it's one of the best things you can do for your heart right now.

If you have solid friendships already, there's benefit in sticking with them, in continuing with those who know your situation and love you. But there's also benefit in finding a group of new friends who don't know your past and can be an outlet for a fresh start. The ideal is both!

Here's the thing. Finding new friends in this season can bring three helpful realizations for your heart.

1. All change isn't bad. (Because it isn't.)
2. Good things can come from bad circumstances. (Because they will.)
3. You're still likable and worthy of love. (Because you are.)

Allow me to tell you another tale.

Many moons ago, when we were first married, my ex-husband and I joined a local gym. There was a trainer there named Jonathan whom we both formed a friendship with. As time marched on, we had to drop our membership and Jonathan moved elsewhere in his fitness instruction journey. The friendship understandably drifted away.

Fast-forward to the year before my husband left. Jonathan contacted me out of the blue via social media and explained he was helping launch a ministry for young adults and asked if my husband and I would like to get involved. I wanted to but felt awkward knowing the rocky state of our marriage, which wasn't public knowledge. It felt hypocritical to work with and influence young people as a husband-and-wife team when I wasn't even sure where my husband stood spiritually anymore. I politely and reluctantly declined, but the invitation lingered in my mind.

Several months later, my husband left. Jonathan once again invited me to that group that had formed, now named Authentic Ministries. Remember the ministry I mentioned in chapter 6, led by Bobby? They were getting together for pizza, and he thought I should come meet everyone and get connected. I hesitantly agreed.

Then I almost didn't go.

After all, I was tired. I was insecure. I had nothing to wear. I didn't even particularly like the pizza at this particular restaurant (too gourmet).

But I went. And God changed my life.

I ate pizza with them, so clueless in the moment to the way God was about to radically knock my socks off because of those very people sitting around me, scarfing down pepperoni thin crust and sweet tea. I don't remember the exact moment our acquaintanceship turned into a fiercely loyal, siblings-in-Christ, ride-or-die level of friendship, but it was a gift straight from heaven.

I think back to that night and shudder to consider what paths I might have taken had Jonathan not invited me (twice!) to that group. Had group leaders Bobby and Christy not scooped this hurting single mama under their widespread wings. Had J-Mick and Christa and "Dale" and Natasha and Hallie and so many others not come alongside me, accepting me as their own despite my being several years older. Despite my being "the divorced one," they loved on me, loved on my young daughter, and will forever be part of the tribe I carry in my heart.

It sounds dramatic, but I'm actually holding back here. I just wish I could help you grasp the importance of it all through these pages.

Think about it. Is there an invitation you're sitting on because you "have nothing to wear"? Is there a ministry you're wanting to get plugged into but think you're no longer qualified for because of your divorce? A Bible study that's starting? A new MOPS group?

Is there a woman at church you thought about introducing yourself to but chickened out last minute because you assume your life is too drama filled right now for anything new?

Are you dodging potential outings and events and connections out of fear of being cast aside and rejected?

What if they're your Bobby and Christy?

What if that group is your Authentic Ministry?

What if That Thing you're avoiding or That Person you're dodging is the refill to your cup?

Please don't miss out. Go anyway. Go scared, go insecure, go even if you don't like the food. (Ha!) Put yourself out there to be blessed.

If you haven't received any invitations and don't have any inklings of people to meet—then pray and ask the Lord to bring them to you. Then go to church, to the gym, to the parent board at the school. Make yourself available. I have personally witnessed so many answered prayers when it comes to friendship—not only for me, but for my daughter. God knows we are people of community, and I believe he has a community for you. But unless your tribe happens to be takeout drivers, you're going to have to make some effort.

> **God knows we are people of community, and he has a community for you.**

Because I accepted Jonathan's invitation, I met the group who taught me so much about the Holy Spirit. The group who stretched me out of my comfort zone and challenged me in ways that filled me to overflowing. The group that taught me to be bold, to pray over strangers, to dive further into the Word, to witness in retail stores, to give generously and without hesitation. To worship freely.

To do it all scared.

Authentic—that little group of young adults, ranging in age from eighteen to thirtyish—was the answer to a prayer I hadn't even prayed. Over those next few years, we met weekly for Bible study and fellowship. We prayed over strangers in Target and held fundraisers so we could bless people at the grocery store by spontaneously paying for their groceries. We performed skits on college stages and held community worship nights and downtown prayer walks through the city. We dreamed big and played hard and loved much, and my faith—much like the Grinch's heart—grew "three sizes" that season, one hug, one prayer session, one worship song at a time.

When I was with my tribe in Authentic, I didn't feel quite so single. They reminded me of the purpose God had for my life that went well beyond earthly marriage (which is where my vision tended to get stuck). They were there for me through my dating attempts, reminding me of my worth and value in Christ when I faltered and holding my arms up when I grew weary of the journey.

I can't believe I could have missed it.

I'm so glad I did it scared.

Bobby and Christy ended up moving their family out of state a few months after I married my new husband. I stayed in Louisiana with my husband, while they church-planted on the East Coast. It was the end of that chapter in my life and the beginning of another—the passing of a baton, so to speak. And that little group called Authentic is now a growing church in Hickory, North Carolina. None of us really knew the plans the Lord had for any of us that night at pizza, corporately and individually.

And you don't know either.

But God promises big things. "Now to him who is able to do far more abundantly than all that we ask or think, according to the power at work within us, to him be glory in the church and in Christ Jesus throughout all generations, forever and ever. Amen" (Ephesians 3:20–21).

If that doesn't just slap you across the face with hope!

One of the themes of this book, as you've probably realized, is hope for your never-ending story. Some chapters in life are downright rough, aren't they? But some are so precious, so treasured, and so valuable. Don't miss the good moments because you're afraid to turn the page.

Do it scared.

Chapter 21

God Heals in Mysterious Ways

IN AN EARLIER CHAPTER, I talked about how we think we know what God is doing, but we often guess completely wrong. We can even get arrogant in our predictions. We think it's so obvious and we have it all figured out and know exactly what's happening.

As a novelist, I feel like I'm especially prone to that frequent misinterpretation of God's work in my life, because it's literally my job to create and project what-ifs into the world. That makes for good stories but rather bad theology.

The truth is, we rarely have God, *or* his plans, figured out in advance. And I'm grateful we don't—because God's ways are so much better than ours. Since our healing from divorce typically takes place along the journey, we'd miss out on a lot of life and blessings if we knew the end from the beginning. We'd be in such a rush to get there, we'd neglect the growth along the way. As hard as it is, it's best to trust that to the Lord's sovereignty.

A few years before my husband left, I attended an annual writers' conference through American Christian Fiction Writers (ACFW). This was when I was still trying to break into traditional publishing houses and had written a young adult novel set in a beach town. At this conference, there were a lot of opportunities to try to sell your current manuscript to agents and editors in the industry, and we were always taught to "be ready to pitch at all times." Not nerve-racking at all, right?

Trying to do me a favor, a sweet friend grabbed my arm after a class and pulled me over to meet the publisher of Thomas Nelson—one of the biggest fiction houses in the industry. "Tell Allen what you're working on," she commanded.

I'm not sure which shook worse—my hands or my voice—as I pitched my story to this important executive. He was kind and gracious, despite the minor train wreck that was my story idea, and I remember naively thinking, *This is it!* I thought meeting the publisher of such a prestigious house would be the start of my journey to publication. It was so obvious. Surely that random, sudden introduction had a grand purpose.

One year later, and I was back at the same conference, my marriage secretly hanging by a thread and my focus far from my publication goals. I attended a workshop taught by Allen and an up-and-coming fiction author Jim, and something happened that I'll never forget. They passed out composition notebooks to every attendee, each notebook containing a handwritten note they had prayed about in advance before writing. Not knowing who was getting which notebook, they simply trusted the Holy Spirit to make sure the right message reached the right attendee.

My handwritten message registered deeply, and I spent the majority of that class time fighting back tears and reveling in awe over how the Lord was working on my behalf. Afterward, my heart pounding, I took a chance and told Allen and Jim what I was walking through in my marriage and how much the notebook and the class content had ministered to my heart.

I can still hear the rush of wind as they scooped me under their proverbial wings and proceeded to walk my divorce journey with me as mentors and prayer warriors.

I'm so glad I had no idea what God was doing. I'm so glad all those years ago, when I thought meeting Allen was a providential ticket to publication, that I was incredibly off the mark. I'm eternally grateful the Lord had bigger plans than my finite mind could have ever imagined.

Everything works so much better when we surrender to his timetable. Just like you can't rush healing a broken leg, you can't rush healing your broken heart. Stay in your cast for the time being. The healing *is* happening, even on the days you can't think past the ache.

Trust the process.

> **Everything works so much better when we surrender to God's timetable.**

That day when I awkwardly pitched that poor YA novel (which still hasn't seen a bookshelf and probably never will), I had no idea I was about to have a need that went so much deeper and broader than a desire to be published. Never could I have imagined what God was up to even in those early moments, preparing the tribe that would walk with me and help lift my arms in my toughest season. They were the flashlights the Lord shined at my feet when my path looked exceedingly dark. If you have those people on your journey, please take a moment and recognize them for what they are—a gift from God. And if you don't have those people right now, they could be right around the corner. Even now as I write this paragraph, I'm praying God sends them to uplift you and ultimately show his lavish love for you.

He's already working behind the scenes for you too. I know it's hard to grasp right now, but one day, in the not-so-far future, you'll see your own stories. You'll see those fingerprints of the Lord all over your recent past, and your mouth will drop with awe. Your heart will swell and sing.

You'll feel that hope soar and dip and rise to heights you never thought you'd feel again.

Now, stay with me. It gets even cooler.

"Coincidentally," that same year, Allen stepped down from traditional publishing to work in media and content at Ransomed Heart Ministries in Colorado, now known as Wild at Heart after the well-known men's book of the same name by John Eldredge. (John and his wife, Stasi, cowrote a female equivalent titled *Captivating*.) Wild at Heart offered semiannual retreats that focused on teaching and worship, addressed inner wounds, and ultimately hoped to restore men's hearts to the Lord and lead them into a deeper walk with him.

That's the retreat on the West Coast that my ex attended right before he left me—the one I mentioned in chapter 1.

Allen was there that week, working. Jim was there, attending.

They got to meet him.

Pray for him and over him.

Pour into him.

Once again, I was so sure I knew what God was up to. So did they. We thought God had brought my ex to my friends and mentors to heal our marriage. But as you remember from prior chapters, it didn't go as planned. My ex came home from California and left me that same night.

But this is where it gets cool . . .

The Lord didn't allow me a single drop of bitterness. It would have been so easy to write off the entire ministry as a fraud, or project blame onto the leadership there, or wallow in what should have happened. My husband was supposed to come home fixed. He was supposed to be healed and fall in love with me all over again.

But there was no bitterness in my heart. You know what the Lord did?

He plunked me on a plane one month later to that same retreat, this time for women, and this time held in Fraser, Colorado. And at that camp, with snow drifts up to my hips and golden aspens dancing all around me, I experienced healing in a fresh way. My inner wounds were addressed. My heart was restored to the Lord.

And I did it scared. I was scared of flying, scared of leaving my young daughter with my parents when there was so much upheaval in her little life. Scared of reaching out for healing, because what if it just hurt even more? But the Lord beckoned, made a way financially and emotionally, and off I went.

At the Captivating retreat, I worshipped with roughly four hundred other women, all of whom were facing their own trials. I made dear heart-friends that I keep up with today. I learned how to pray and intercede for others in new ways. I journaled and wept and watched the aspens wave their golden hands and felt closer to God than I had in years.

I was healing. It hurt, yes. Every diary entry was dotted black with mascara-laden tears. There were evenings when my throat hurt from singing as loud as I could to drown out the enemy's lies. There was a deep ache in my heart that throbbed raw and real.

But I was healing.

Sometimes God uses unwanted circumstances in our lives—even divorce—to develop us into who we're meant to be. To prepare us for the things he has for us.

I recently came across the concept of *telos*, which is an ancient Greek term used by Aristotle that refers to fulfillment.[1] The end. Completion of purpose. That stuck with me because I can so clearly see God working toward my own *telos*. Using all things for good, à la Romans 8:28.

He's doing that for you too. I'm not some weird exception to the rule. He loves you, and he has a plan through all this grit and despair you're wading through. It won't be wasted, and it won't be without *telos*. If I hadn't gone through this divorce season, I wouldn't be who

I am today. I wouldn't have the faith I have. I wouldn't have the scars and (literal) tattoos testifying to his goodness.

I'd have missed a lot. And so would you.

> **Sometimes God uses unwanted circumstances in our lives—even divorce— to develop us into who we're meant to be. To prepare us for the things he has for us.**

None of that experience—from first meeting Allen at the writers' conference, to the special notebooks, to the powerful worship sessions at Captivating—looked the way I once pictured. But the Lord graciously allowed me, via the precious gift of hindsight, to see how big that picture really was. How far it extended. How wide and broad and deep it stretched (sort of like his love for us). And I'm sure one day in eternity we'll look back and see all those puzzle pieces put together.

But for now, I can attest that the Lord heals in mysterious ways. While my ex was supposed to be the one restored, the Lord had healing for me all along. He met me in those tree-dotted mountains, sat with me while I gulped cups of the best apple cider I've ever had to date, and brought comfort I didn't know was possible.

It's possible for you too. Right now, you might be thinking your ache will never end. You might be feeling like this is how it's going to be for the rest of your life, and you have to find a way to deal with it. That's not true, friend. I'm living proof. Time didn't heal me. Getting remarried to a wonderful man years later didn't heal me.

The Lord healed me.

And he used publishers, composition notebooks, best-selling authors, worship songs, snow-covered leaves, and apple cider to do it. He used a bumpy plane ride, inspired teaching, tear-stained diaries, and new friendships. He used prayer warriors and sore throats and overpacked suitcases, and his very own presence. Mostly he used my unfulfilled expectations.

What is he using for you?

Look around. It's there. Maybe for you, he's using a once-dormant dream to breathe fresh passion into your heart. Or adopted animals, sticky hugs from your kids, classic movies, and old worship songs. Or he's using women's retreats and football games and reunions with high school besties.

But he's always, always using his presence. His presence is life.

Remember, the healing comes in layers. I wasn't done healing at Captivating, but a significant portion of that initial pain was dealt with in those snow-dusted cabins in Fraser. It was broken off and buried in the mountains beneath the aspens.

You might think you haven't made any progress because it still hurts, but if you look again, you'll see the transformation. You'll see how you're growing stronger every week, how the Lord is sustaining you even though some days it feels a lot like plucking manna from the ground—bare minimum. Scarcity instead of abundance.

But your life and faith won't stay that way forever. Healing builds from the inside out. One layer is dealt with at a time, just as a deep cut that requires stitches takes weeks and months to heal. Just like a broken bone takes time. The Lord is working in your heart, layer by layer.

One betrayal, one fear, one insecurity at a time.

Over the next several years of annual ACFW conferences, I would update Allen and Jim on my progress. We'd sit in the lobby and drink coffee and discuss what God was up to—especially in my dating life, which was usually a hot mess. Until one special year, when I came back and got to introduce them to my new husband. That time, we sat, drank coffee, and celebrated as we talked about how good God was. How intentional. And yet how very unpredictable.

Sometimes, you think God is introducing you to a publisher to pitch your story, then you realize he's actually rewriting your life story. And still other times, you look over and see your new husband reading Jim's latest novel on your anniversary beach trip, and you just shake your head in wonder. God can—and does—restore in the coolest, weirdest, most (seemingly) random ways. He's got you.

So don't give up hope. Don't think God's done with your story or your pain. Don't think there's only hurt ahead.

The best is yet to come.

Chapter 22

Dating as a Single Parent
(aka Hula-Hooping with Barbed Wire)

IN MY DIVORCE JOURNEY, I learned three truths.

1. Dating is hard.
2. Dating as a woman in her thirties is really hard.
3. Dating as a single mom in her thirties is akin to Hula-Hooping with barbed wire.

I'm not trying to discourage you, but to prepare you. When I started dating again, I was roughly a decade out from my first date with my ex-husband—and I realized quickly that a lot had changed in that ten-year span. For example, technology had significantly advanced. Dating apps had become a popular thing, as had social media. You didn't just meet someone at church or work, like you did in my day—you had to go find them. Digitally. And hope it clicked in person at that first coffee date and that they weren't a serial killer.

Okay, maybe that's a little dramatic, but not by much. I have stories.

But first, there's a conversation begging to be had.

If you need to ask the question, "Am I ready to date?" the answer is most likely no. It's one of those things you instinctively recognize in your gut. If you're wondering if you're ready, then you're picking up on some cue deep inside your heart that's waving its arms, hopping around with Band-Aids and bruises while shouting, "Not yet!"

But if you're like me, you're going to do it anyway because some things you have to learn the hard way. Plenty of godly, wise people counseled me against dating before I was legally divorced. And they were right.

I should have waited.

I can think of one person who did wait until after becoming legally divorced, and her life has been so full of peace and blessing. She was abandoned by a spouse who cheated on her and who moved on immediately, and yet my friend stayed the course. Continued wearing her ring. Didn't even change her social media status to single. She was still technically married, so she carried out her vows until the divorce was official.

That's so rare, and yet so wise.

It's truly the right idea, not only morally, but emotionally. If the covenant has been broken through adultery or your spouse has abandoned you and you know there is no hope of reconciliation—perhaps he's already moved on and is dating or even engaged again—you might logically think, "What's the difference if I start seeking a new relationship now or after my court date?" After all, if the marriage is over and broken before God, then what's the big deal in waiting for it to be legal with the state?

I thought the same thing, and I was wrong.

Being aboveboard and following the rules God gives is in our own best interest and for our protection. You don't want to hear that, and I didn't either. But I know now it's true. If you're married, you're *not* single or available for a new relationship. It's that simple. (I said simple, not easy.) We've all known people who rushed from one dating relationship to another, with barely enough time in between for a new TV episode to come out, let alone for a heart to fully heal, and we raise our eyebrows at the wisdom in that. We assume rebound and expect the new relationship to not do well. Usually, we are right.

How much more so when it comes to a marriage ending?

Not only is waiting to date taking the high road and morally appropriate before God, but also waiting protects you emotionally. When you date before you're divorced, there is no chance that your heart is ready for the jump. You're still recovering from the previous fall. Your adrenaline hasn't even faded yet!

> **Not only is waiting to date taking the high road and morally appropriate before God, but also waiting protects you emotionally.**

You might think, "Well, we had kids and were already required to wait a year while we were separated and in proceedings, so this doesn't apply to me."

Trust me, it applies to you.

You're not ready.

I know you want to be ready. I know you think you're ready. But until the paperwork has been processed and your heart is fully healed, it's not time to take the leap.

And that, dear reader, is where the "do as I say, not as I do" portion of this book begins.

My first date after I realized my marriage was over was interesting to say the least. He was a sweet guy, an acquaintance of a mutual friend but a stranger to me, and he picked me up from work in his truck. We went to dinner at a nice restaurant and walked around the scenic grounds, then headed off to see a movie. He was polite. Respectful. Engaging.

Yet the entire experience felt surreal. Instead of focusing on getting to know him as a person or trying to make a new friend, I could only think of how off the entire experience was. It wasn't his fault—it was mine.

I wasn't ready.

Then at the movie theater, he generously bought us a popcorn to share (totally fine!) and one drink . . . with two straws. The gesture felt abruptly intimate. I know he had no intention of that and was just trying to save money (which I completely respect), but it showed I wasn't ready. For any of it.

After saying goodbye and thanking him for a lovely evening (and appreciating the fact that he didn't try to kiss me), I went home and bawled.

But instead of realizing the simple truth—that I wasn't ready to date—I assumed the disconnect came from attempting to date an essential stranger. So next, I chose to get involved with someone I already knew through multiple channels. It felt much safer.

Turns out, it was one of the more dangerous things I've done. My heart, not fully healed (or even halfway healed), clung to that dysfunctional relationship like a barnacle to an anchor. And to further the nautical analogy, I became like a ship going down—fast. That relationship carried me under the waves, and every time I tried to get out of it, my insecurities and low self-esteem tugged me right back down. I was caught in a stronghold and was turning into a person I didn't recognize. I did things I swore I never would. I drifted from God out of an underlying urge to solve my own problems instead of waiting on his timing.

And I paid for it, dearly.

There were two instrumental factors that helped liberate me from that undertow. The first occurred one night while I was taking a shower. Alone with my thoughts, I couldn't escape the reality of what my life had become. Part of me wanted to do the right thing—the God-honoring, hard thing—and end the relationship. But part of me didn't want to let go of the new familiar, toxic as it was, that I had become dependent on. That relationship had become a piece of driftwood, and I was clinging to it with all my might.

Letting go and holding on felt equally risky.

I tried to pray about it but felt so guilty from my current decisions and lifestyle I couldn't find the words. Instead, as the water ran cold, the Holy Spirit impressed upon me the reminder that I was loved. And that we would deal with my sin later. But as his child, I needed to first remember how very wanted and accepted and chosen I was. That assurance had to come first in order to give me the courage to do the next step.

That truth of being loved settled deep inside, slowly pushing out the condemnation, and was the first key to my becoming set free. It didn't happen immediately. But not long after, the second key clicked in the lock—accountability.

I knew my weakness, so when the opportunity arose, I went to my current pastor and his wife and confessed everything. I asked for prayer and help, and they gave it. They told me hard truths to my face, with love and a lot of hugs. They prayed over me, then told me to do the right thing and that it'd be worth it.

Knowing I had their support, I ended the relationship. And knowing I was answering to them in the aftermath, I was able to keep my distance from the guy involved and let things fully die.

It wasn't easy. One night, I had a throbbing headache and wanted someone to take care of me. I wanted to feel seen and be noticed and, most of all, not be alone. I sent an SOS text to my friend who had come to the monastery with me the prior year.

> Help. I'm going to call him.
> I'm going to cave.

> No you won't.

She was at my apartment door within the hour with headache meds, Chex Mix, and an icy can of soda—her personal cure-all for a migraine. She stayed with me until I felt stronger, both physically and spiritually, and the temptation passed.

I never called him.

The stronghold was broken. And one year later, I took a chocolate-covered fruit basket up to the church office to thank my pastor and his wife for their role in leading me back to the Lord.

If you're trying to date too soon, I'm sure one of these situations is familiar in its own way for you. You probably well know the pitfalls of strongholds, of temptation, of trying to heal yourself with tools that only proceed to cut you deeper. Of knowing something isn't the right fit for you but being so afraid there won't be something else later. (I won't even get into my brief stint with trying out nightclubs. Oy.)

It's all a trust issue, and when you've walked through a divorce, you understandably have several.

So how do you know when you *are* ready to grab that ring of barbed wire and start dating again? Here are five check marks that might help you evaluate your heart.

1. *You are legally divorced.* (I won't elaborate on this again, but please know, it's *got* to come first!)
2. *You're not seeking attention from every man you encounter.* This isn't to say you're never going to crave a second glance or appreciate a head turn when it happens. But you know the difference—you're appreciating being asked out or noticed, but that isn't the goal when you walk into a room.
3. *You're not giving off "Are you my future husband?" vibes.* Like my point above, you know what this feels like. In the height of my lonely healing process, I practically pulsed cartoon heart eyes at every single guy I saw within my age range. I had become a rather disturbing, real-life example of the famous children's book

by P. D. Eastman, *Are You My Mother?* Except instead of a bird, I was a broken woman, silently asking, "Are you my husband?" Learn from me. Don't be that overeager little bird woman.

4. *You're not consumed with the thought of dating.* When you're ready to date, you're not worried about whether you do. Dating becomes almost an afterthought. Maybe it's a goal in your life, but it's not the end-all goal. It's not your main concern. Your focus is more on your walk with God, your children, your church, your hobbies, your career, and everything else that makes up your blessed, full life—rather than being hyper-focused on "I need a man."

5. *You're content with the Lord.* This doesn't mean you aren't still desiring marriage or hoping for a companion one day, but your soul is content in your walk with God. It is well with your soul. You have days where the lonely hits harder, but overall, you feel stable. You have a full life outside of dating, a life you truly love and enjoy. You're open to more, but not demanding it with panic. You've realized you're not incomplete when you're single. You're full in Christ.

Of course, none of the suggestions above guarantee a relationship, and they certainly don't mean everything will be hunky-dory. In fact, you'd think I would have learned my lesson after my first failed attempts, but it took just a little longer to get it right. Because I was still healing from my wounds and still a little broken, I attracted broken men who also were looking to depend on me in ways I couldn't maintain. There were seasons I felt like I must have been holding up a neon sign that blasted, "TOXIC RELATIONSHIP SEEKERS APPLY HERE."

I learned the hard lessons a little more quickly in those years, though not always quickly enough. For example, I learned that men who are insecure when you go out with friends for an evening instead of with them aren't healthy and ready for a relationship. Men who buy you jewelry and then give you the cold shoulder if you don't wear it every single day aren't healthy and ready for a relationship. Men who hear you say you want to set physical boundaries but then pressure you for sex aren't healthy and ready for a relationship. And men who lead you on for eight months but refuse to ever meet your daughter (or refuse to let you meet their children) aren't healthy and ready for a relationship.

I learned that men who sit next to you in a restaurant but hold their phone *waaaaay* over there every time a text notification dings are unhealthy. Men who offer lip service to the Lord but are unrepentant for their sin are unhealthy. Men who guest preach a sermon on a Sunday and then try to convince you to spend a week with them in a hotel in Dallas afterward are unhealthy.

All those events and their baggage nearly convinced me to cancel my first date with my now-husband. We were both so over the dating game when we connected online. We were tired of trying. We hadn't given up completely, but we were a hair away from thinking we would just be single the rest of our lives. We were over the anticipation, the hope, the letdown, the games . . . It all felt like an inevitable cycle, and we were burned out. It was easier at that point not to try.

The Hula-Hoop of barbed wire had left its scars, and we wanted to set it down for good.

But we went to coffee anyway.

I remember anxiously waiting inside my favorite coffee shop for him to drive the forty-five minutes from his home to meet me. I was wearing a new purple shirt and ordered a white-chocolate mocha. He walked in with skinny jeans and a great haircut, and we immediately realized we had things in common. Our young daughters. Our love for God. A heart for worship. We were both artists in our own way—he was a drummer, and I wrote books. We had families who loved us and supported us. We'd both been abandoned in a divorce we didn't ask for but that had happened nonetheless. And we recognized that we'd both grown in our faith and in our walks with God because of it.

Despite all the odds stacked against us in our past, we had a fresh hope.

Maybe we were finally ready.

That white-chocolate-mocha date led to him proposing five months later and me walking the aisle four months after that. I'll never forget how holy our wedding ceremony felt. The pastor who prayed, "Let it be," over me the prior year performed the ceremony, and we took Communion instead of lighting a unity candle. Friends from every season of my life were in attendance, celebrating God's work of redemption and restoration. Beauty from ashes. Beauty from the broken. My life had become a giant masterpiece of mosaic tiles.

That's not to say it's been perfect ever since, or even easy. Blending families, stepparenting, and remarriage have their own challenges. Nothing is perfect this side of heaven. But it's a gift. It's a provision. It's a beautiful work in progress.

My victory over divorce was *not* in getting remarried. That was a blessing, yes. But my truest, deepest, most authentic post-divorce victory came from being able to tell this full testimony to the glory of God.

I made mistakes. I didn't walk it perfectly. It was a painful, confusing season.

But I'm grateful for it.

Whatever your specific situation is regarding your own marriage, whether you had to leave or were left, you also won't walk this out perfectly. But you have a testimony to give.

So now I ask you—what is that testimony going to look like when it's all said and done?

You might experience a similar story of remarriage like mine one day. You might reconcile with your ex and have a miracle testimony. You might stay single and honor God with your life that way. Or you might meet your future husband tomorrow. The point is, you don't know, and making unhealthy, desperate attempts to force something to happen isn't going to give you peace. Remarriage isn't the cure-all or end-all. So stop striving toward a goal that won't fulfill you or solve your aching heart problems. Let it happen.

"Let it be."

I know that's hard to surrender. I have a vivid memory of walking through the appliance and home store I used to work at, having just ended yet another toxic relationship, and thinking, *This is impossible.* How in the world was I going to meet anyone? Ending the relationship that needed ending left me with no real prospects for the future. But beneath that wave of despair lay an anchor of sturdy hope—it wasn't up to me. It was up to God. God had a million creative ways of potentially bringing my future spouse into my life, and I didn't have to be the one to try to figure it out.

He ended up doing it through Facebook and a mutual friend of all things.

The only way I can explain it is that one day I was single, and the next day I was in a relationship. One day I didn't know my husband, and the next day I did. It happened that quickly and was pretty much out of my control. In a million years, I couldn't have arranged all the details that led to my husband and me meeting any more than I could throw a lasso around the moon or breathe fire.

It can easily be the same for you. God knows the plan, so all you need to do is focus on the next thing. Living out your responsibilities right now, where you are, and doing them well and for the glory of God. Working for the Lord. Raising your kids for the Lord. Honoring your walk with him and your purity and your reputation. Growing closer to Christ and building your trust in his provision and faithfulness. Focus your attention and energy and efforts there.

Matthew 6:33 (NLT) says, "Seek the Kingdom of God above all else, and live righteously, and he will give you everything you need."

If you walk closely with God and stop trying to force your way into a relationship or marriage again, you'll have rest—whether you ever remarry or not. Trusting and surrendering bring peace. Trying to control everything brings anxiety.

The details of how two people meet and start dating are usually never quite as expected. There's no formula to finding a godly spouse. It's all a big question mark. But one thing I do know—your hope, joy, and peace are not found in dating, marriage, or remarriage. Relationships will come and go, and they can't be forced or controlled. That's the hard news.

The good news is that the only sustainable hope, joy, and peace we could ever possibly have are already ours for the taking, in Christ alone.

Don't date before you are ready.

Don't fall for the lie that you have to marry again to be whole.

Don't think being single means you aren't valuable or desirable.

Don't believe your future is hopeless.

And don't, for even a moment, think you are alone for a single step of the journey.

> **The only sustainable hope, joy, and peace we could ever possibly have are already ours for the taking, in Christ alone.**

I see you, but more importantly, the God of the universe sees you and beckons you to him. He made a way for relationship with you through his Son. Jesus, who came and lived a perfect life in the midst of all our imperfections, who knew the sin you would one day commit and took it upon himself on the cross anyway, died and rose again to forge a forever home with you.

God loved you that much.

Your spouse might have failed you. But God never, ever will. Even now he's working things out for your good. Your spouse might not have realized the treasure you are, but God created you in his own image. Your spouse might have betrayed you, but God is forever faithful. Your spouse might have shattered your heart, but God is near to the brokenhearted. He's real.

He's not a fairy tale. He's so much better.

Your story isn't over yet, friend. And with Christ, there's a happily ever after directly in reach.

A Prayer for You, Dear Reader

Dear God,

Grasp the hand of the sweet woman holding these pages and tug her closer to you. Cover her with your wings. Tuck her into your heart. Let her feel your presence in fresh ways as she moves forward in her journey.

Remind her, Lord, that she is never alone, never forgotten, and is forever fully seen by you. We live in a fallen world, and people will disappoint us. But you, Lord, are eternal. You are good. You are trustworthy.

Spouses may lie to us, but Scripture tells us that Jesus is the way, the truth, and the life. Spouses might leave, but we trust where your Word says you never forsake us.

Spouses change, but you, God, are blessedly the same—yesterday and today and tomorrow.

Thank you for this dear woman, Father. Draw her closer. Let the assurance of your love and the gospel shout louder and ring truer than any lie from the enemy.

If she feels left behind, hold her hand and pull her into step with you.

If she feels forgotten, sing over her with your mighty song.

If she feels lost, light her path with your love and your Word.

If she feels heartbroken, let her remember you are near to her.

If she feels shame, tell her there is no condemnation for those in Christ.

And as she feels the deep sting of divorce, remind her that you, her Maker, are her husband.

Amen.

Acknowledgments

You might have heard it said, "Writing a book takes a village." But it feels like this one took an entire galaxy! I'd be remiss if I didn't acknowledge a few of those shining stars.

To my agent—Tamela Hancock Murray. You believed in me many moons ago, and didn't freak out when I emailed you a nonfiction proposal with zero heads-up. Thanks for continuing to support and encourage me at every step of this writing journey.

To Megan—If not for you, I'd probably still be in the fetal position under my desk. Your prayers and friendship help me shine! You're a gift.

To Stacey—Thanks for praying with me through this process, and checking in with me every Sunday. That meant so much!

To Mammaw Jo and Granddaddy, both now in heaven—you prayed for me and with me during my divorce season. Thanks for circling with me around your living room and holding my hands tight while we went to our Father. I'll never forget those moments.

To author Mary DeMuth—You probably don't even remember this, but a long time ago, you sat with me at a table during a meal at ACFW Conference and heard part of my story, then casually suggested I write a nonfiction book. This is your fault, really.

To Janyre—You saw potential in this book when others didn't, and made it happen. Thanks for walking with me through every step! And to the editorial and marketing teams at Kregel . . . big hugs. Thank you for partnering with me to get this book out. You all made it stronger.

To my parents—I never would have survived that dark season without you both. Thanks for supporting me emotionally, helping me financially, coparenting with me when I felt alone, and reminding me I never was.

And to Topher—I'm so grateful that my story wasn't over, and that ours is newly begun.

(Also special thanks to my dog, who checked on me when I typed "The End" on this manuscript and then fell facedown on the floor and didn't move for ten minutes.)